DATING

A Guide to **Creating** Intimate Relationships

Daniel Linder

Copyright @1992 by Daniel Linder
All rights reserved including the right of reproduction in whole or in part in any form.

Library of Congress Catalog Card Number 93-90552
ISBN Number 0-9639565-0-7

Hylen Publishing
935 Lootens, Suite 208
San Rafael, CA 94901
Tel. (415) 456-0802

Dedicated to my uncle, Henry Goldwurm

Foreward

In American culture, dating is the vehicle for the selection of a mate. Through the process of dating, selections are made that enable the creation of new families.

The foundation of the family is the couple relationship. The more secure, the more intimate, the more loving the couple, the more functional the family will be.

The couple must operate in a context of integrity, one that promotes trust and safety in order for the essential ingredient of intimacy to develop. This begins the moment two people begin to relate to each other and continues to develop throughout the relationship. If the relationship develops in a context of deception, mistrust and manipulation, it is unlikely that a trusting, bonded relationship will emerge. Conversely, if the relationship begins within a context of honesty and integrity, an opportunity will exist to create a trusting, loving relationship.

In "Dating: A Guide to Creating Intimate Relationships," the process of developing a healthy relationship is detailed. Elements essential to an intimate and trusting relationship are identified and carefully examined, providing a map to one of the most important journeys of our lives: the selection of a mate. If we as a culture are to survive and flourish, we must recognize the importance of dating and not treat it as if it were a natural, innate process. Successful dating requires insight into the essential ingredients of healthy relating. Tools need to be developed to help promote an environment of relating that can allow the flourishing of healthy, loving, intimate relationships. Dating is often an uncomfortable and awkward experience. The American culture's lack of acknowledgment of the significance of this essential developmental experience and its failure to provide appropriate education to enhance this process have contributed to these feelings. This book both acknowledges the importance of dating as a developmental milestone and provides an educational framework in which dating can culminate in a lasting intimate relationship.

Neil Kobrin, M.D.

Dr. Kobrin is a clinical psychologist and the president of California Graduate School of Psychology, a professional graduate school in Corte Madera, California, that offers master's and doctoral degrees in clinical psychology emphasizing family systems. He maintains a private practice in Mill Valley, where he provides psychotherapy for couples, families and individuals.

Acknowledgments

There are several people in this world to whom I am grateful for making this book possible. First of all, I would like to thank my parents who, as two people who have stayed happily together for nearly fifty years, serve as role models of a quality relationship. Without their love for each other and their love for me, I doubt I would have had the many rich learning experiences in relationships upon which the principles of this book are based.

I wish to acknowledge and thank all those people who participated in the **Dating To Relate** workshops for believing in my vision, and also for their willingness to give so much of themselves during the many intense, demanding evenings the workshops took place.

Furthermore, I would like to thank every client with whom I've shared a therapeutic relationship for experience that would have otherwise been unobtainable.

I am grateful to Rickie Fishman, Richard Flamm, Scott Zagoria, Fran Wickner, Eric Shey, Deanna Washington, Holly Scupp, Mindia Klein, Heidi Swillinger and all others who, at one time or another, have assisted me in the preparation of this book.

A very special acknowledgment is owed to my wife, Barbara, who has always believed in me, and who has supported me in every aspect of my career endeavors. Without her, I would not have had the strong, stable family life that nourishes me when I come home feeling depleted, and which gives my life meaning and purpose. She's my life-partner, best friend and mother to my two sons.

CONTENTS

Introduction 1

PART ONE: BUILDING INTIMATE RELATIONSHIPS 4

1 The Challenge of a Lifetime 5
   Why Do We Date? 5
   What Is an Intimate Relationship? 6
   Dysfunctional vs. Functional Relationships 8
   Relationships Are Created 9
   Gaining the Necessary Experience 11
2 Happily Ever Now 13
   What Is a Date? 13
   Being in the Moment 14
   Great Expectations 15
   The Best and Worst That Can Happen 16
   "Dating Partnership" 22
   Prepare for the Future, Handle the Moment 23
3 "The Writing Is on the Wall" 25
   Misconceptions 25
   Conflict Has Its Place 27
   Avoid Now, Pay Later 30
   The "Ninety-nine Percent" Phenomenon 31
   Exercise: The Writing on the Wall 32
4 The "Clean Slate" 33
   Emotional Baggage From Prior Relationships 33
   Rejected Once Again 35
   "No One's Really Interested" 36
   Preconceived Notions 37
   Don't Limit Your Options! 44
5 Rapport: A Joint-Effort Creation 45
   Intimacy Begins With Rapport 45
   The Personalization Phenomenon 46
   If You Need to Know, You Better Find Out! 47
   Handling Criticism -- and Compliments 48
6 Polishing Your Communication Skills 54
   How Do You Generate Rapport? 54
   Awareness Is Your Guide 55
   Knowing When You're Disrespected 55
   Getting to Know You: Self-Disclosure 60
   What and How Much Information Should You Disclose? 61

Why Can't You Read My Mind?	62
Asking Usually Means You're Interested	63
Listening	65
"Don't Solve My Problem. Just Listen to Me."	67
Selective Listening	68
So Angry You're No Longer Listening	70

7 Relationships Built to Last 73
- Interest 73
- Honesty 74
- Understanding 76
- A Misunderstanding 78
- Intimacy Works in Mysterious Ways 80
- Intimacy vs. Sexual Attraction 84

8 Rate Your Date: The Ten Critical Questions 87
- Exception to the Rule 95

PART TWO: DEMYSTIFYING SEXUAL ATTRACTION 99

9 Overview of the Most Common Pitfalls 100
- No Attraction, No Interest 100
- Reality Can Be a Drag 101
- Feeling and Acting Are Not the Same 102
- Low Self-Worth 104
- Shame 104
- "Splitting" Sexual and Emotional Intimacy 104
- Sex, Flirting and Romance 108
- Nothing More Than Sex 108
- "Look at Me! I'm Sexy!" 109
- Just You and Me, Forever 110
- Sometimes Learning the Hard Way is the Only Way to Learn 112

10 Cutting Through the Mystique 116
- Our Bodies, Our Sexuality 116
- Our Emotional Needs 117
- Our Imagination 118
- Distinguishing Fantasy From Reality 122
- Exercise: Your Ideal Imaginary Other 129

11 Four Types of Sexual Attraction 131
- Pure Fantasy 131
- Projection of Images 132
- Projection of Emotional Needs 134
- Sexual Attraction as an Outgrowth of Intimacy .. 139

12 For Yourself, By Yourself and With Yourself 143

Appendix 149

INTRODUCTION

When I think about how I felt when I was dating, I wonder why I put myself through such misery. I never wanted to date. I hated the whole process. It was one disappointment after another. I'd spot a woman I was attracted to, then decide I liked her. She would be someone I thought I could connect with on an emotional level, who I would like and who would like me. I was wrong most of the time.

One of the things I never quite figured out was, "How is this woman ever going to see how special and wonderful I am?" With all that I had to offer, to have to go up to her as "just another guy" was humiliating. I was somebody with all these desirable qualities, but when it came to approaching her for a date, I was nobody. I wished there was a way in which we could skip the date -- skip "getting to know each other" -- and somehow, magically perhaps, we would be together at some later stage of relationship. Regardless, there were only two options: either I was going to approach a woman for a date, or I was not ever going to have a girlfriend.

Then there was the date itself to contend with, which was usually worse than having to get the date. I was frequently upset by huge gaps between how I saw myself and how she saw me, between what I imagined it would be like and what it actually was like being with her. Before the date, there was some excitement. After the date, I often wondered, "What happened?! How could I have been so off-track to think about her the way I had?" I alternated between blaming myself, the woman I dated, women in general and the very activity of dating. Whenever I speak to singles, it's immediately apparent that my experience is not at all unusual. I often ask what they consider to be the most uncomfortable aspects of dating. Their responses cover a wide range of issues and complaints:

- "Dating is like being on trial -- only you're guilty until proven innocent! I don't have a chance."

- "Sometimes, when I'm alone, I think about my relationships. I'm quite confused by it all. Who do you trust? Who do you not trust? And what do all the fun and games add up to in the long run, anyway? Sometimes it makes me sad. Sometimes it hurts. Sometimes it makes me angry. Sometimes it makes me numb. Sometimes it makes me sick. I can really get crazy trying to figure it all out."

- "It's like I'm carrying out some kind of agenda to be the 'perfect date,' yet I don't have a clue what that means!"

- "I don't have any problem getting dates. I just don't know how to be spontaneous once I'm out with someone."

- "I never know how my date is feeling."

- "If it's not love at first sight, then why bother?"

- "I seem to always be disappointed. Maybe I'm being unrealistic. Maybe I want too much. But why should I have to settle?"

Both men and women have repeatedly complained about being compared with other people with whom their dates had previously experienced negative or positive relationships. For example, **He**: "If I disagree with her, then all of a sudden I'm just like her father who never listened to her." Or, **She**: "He said I had the same eyes of a past girlfriend. He liked me because I looked like her."

Direction and confidence are lacking while confusion and frustration prevail. The central theme expressed is that, while there is desire to get to know one another and hope to develop an intimate relationship, most people have grown quite discouraged and believe that achieving intimacy and finding the right partner are impossibilities.

Why are relationships such a struggle for so many people? We learn from watching others, most often our friends and family, the majority of whom lack experience in intimate relationships. We also learn from reading books, listening to music and watching movies and television programs. These sources, however, rarely provide depictions of relationships that take us beyond sex, romance and melodrama. They also lead many people to believe that intimacy is much easier to achieve and more common than it actually is, which only reinforces a sense of inadequacy.

There is no guide, no school, no "on the job" training that teaches us **what we need know, what we need to do and how to do it.** DATING is intended to fill that void. With this basic and vital information, you will be able to transform your dating experiences and improve the quality of your relationships.

Part One

BUILDING INTIMATE RELATIONSHIPS

CHAPTER ONE

THE CHALLENGE OF A LIFETIME

Why Do We Date?

For most people, lack of intimacy is an undeniable void. Dating is a means to fill that void.

Of course, developing an intimate relationship is not everyone's primary purpose in dating. People date for a variety of reasons, including loneliness, boredom, need for companionship, to share an activity or to seek romantic and sexual excitement. When any of these reasons are the basis for dating, it is more likely that you will attract a person whose motivation is similar to yours. This sets the stage for short-term, non-intimate relationships. If developing an intimate relationship is not your primary purpose in dating, it is likely you will not find this book particularly useful.

Do we enjoy dating?

If you are like most people, the answer is probably no. We date in hopes of developing an intimate relationship so we no longer have to date. The reality is that there is no way to shortcut the beginning stages of a relationship. Rarely do we go from being single to being in an intimate relationship without expending a lot of time and energy earnestly trying without succeeding.

What Is an Intimate Relationship?

I've heard many people say that they don't know what an intimate relationship is -- that they've never had one and wouldn't know one if it was staring them in the face. Of course it's helpful to have some intimate experiences to fall back on, some point of reference to tell you that you've found what you've been looking for or that at least you're on the right track. However, it isn't actually necessary to have had prior experience in intimate relationships. It is enough to begin with a concept of the kind of relationship you want, of what a healthy, intimate relationship is.

What do you want more than anything else in a relationship? The thousands of responses from those asked this question can be summed up as follows: **trust, acceptance, and respect.**

It is important to understand that **the ability of two people to communicate determines the quality of the relationship they will create.** The more skill they have, the more likely they are to achieve intimacy; the more intimate they become, the longer the relationship is likely to last. There's got to be space for and an ability to work through **negative feelings, conflicts and differences. Common priorities and goals, as well as plans for accomplishing them** must also be established.

What most singles fail to realize is that **the nature of intimacy is one of vulnerability.** Although we wish to feel a sense of control and security in our relationships, the reality is that we ultimately do not have control over what is going to happen and how we are going to feel.

We enter a relationship as two separate people who barely know each other. In the process of learning about each other, we discover that our partners are not who we thought they were, who we thought they should be, who we wish them to be: they're always surprising us. By the same token, we also discover that we are not who we thought we were, who we should or wish to be: we are always surprising ourselves. We might observe things about each other that seem clear and constant, but it's a wholly different matter when conflict occurs. No matter what we do, nothing changes the fact that human beings are limited in more ways than we'd probably care to admit. This is why, during the course of any intimate relationship, we come face to face with our own and our partner's limitations, not once or twice, but dozens of times. No doubt we will find ourselves in situations that go unresolved or are not resolved to our satisfaction, in situations in which we don't know what to do, in which there is anger, fear and every other difficult feeling.

A client (Bill) once asked me, "Is it possible to be intimate without being vulnerable?"

For Bill, the rigors of learning how to communicate intimately with his wife were more than he had bargained for. They required him to open up emotionally, to get in touch with his feelings, to express them and to respond to his wife's expression of her feelings -- altogether new experiences for him! The therapy process forced Bill to examine his long-standing need to protect himself, which he traced back to his abusive relationship with his mother. Having and expressing feelings meant he would be shamed and humiliated. He became more aware of his need to maintain emotional distance in all subsequent relationships, and particularly in his marriage.

For the first time in his life, Bill was being presented with the idea that to be vulnerable means to be emotionally accessible; that there is no way around his feelings and that even though it is unlikely that he will be abused, he is nevertheless vulnerable. His relationship can and should be a refuge from abuse, but it will never be a refuge from vulnerability. It is understanding that he should be seeking, not protection.

The good news was that letting his guard down didn't pose the same threat to his emotional well-being as it had before and that intimacy was within the realm of possibility. The bad news was that he was going to face feelings and issues he felt ill-equipped to deal with.

Bill's experience is representative of the general population. Many of us don't understand the distinction between abuse and vulnerability. We have developed defensive or self-protective behavior patterns and, as a result, are not prepared for the reality of being intimate. We suffer disillusionment and often times feel overwhelmed when we discover our relationships do not provide the safety and security we expected them to.

As we begin to understand and accept that vulnerability is part and parcel of becoming (and staying) intimate, our tolerance for uncomfortable feelings should increase. When we find ourselves in situations in which we feel challenged, we should not only be more inclined to risk ourselves emotionally, we should see these situations as opportunities for growing and deepening our relationships.

Dysfunctional vs. Functional Relationships

A dysfunctional (or unhealthy) relationship is one in which the people involved have entered into the relationship without prior experience in intimate relationships. Their prior experience in relationships taught them that in order to keep the relationship, they must compromise themselves; that relationships are an "**either-or**" **proposition**: if we express our feelings, wants and needs, we will be abandoned (or rejected, ignored, invalidated, etc.), and in order to maintain the relationship, we have to abandon ourselves, which is ultimately what we do when we are children. **Denial is necessary for survival.**

The emotional dynamics of the relationship are shaped by mistrust, self-protection and dependency. Because the tendency is to deny, distort and not express feelings, the hallmark qualities of an intimate relationship -- honesty and vulnerability, understanding, trust, acceptance and respect -- are undeveloped or nonexistent.

In a dysfunctional relationship, there is a lack of a boundary that defines the two people as separate, distinct individuals. They act as a "**we**," not as a "**you**" **and** "**I.**" There is either a merging of identities or a wall that isolates them from one another. There is little ability to communicate about negative feelings, problems, conflicts, differences.

Compare this with a functional relationship in which both people are operating on the basis that there is space to feel and express their true feelings without threat to the relationship, that the relationship can and will survive negative feelings, conflicts and differences. In a functional relationship, in one in which there is intimacy, denial comes at the expense of closeness.

The relationship is based on the "I" **and** "you" concept: the understanding that "what I feel, want and need is going to be different than what you feel, want and need," yet both are valid and equal. Both people treat each other as separate, distinct individuals. Both people effectively communicate about negative feelings, conflicts and differences. Understanding is achieved because they are open about their feelings and desires. Trust and respect are givens. Each person assesses situations in terms of his or her own best interests as well as the best interests of the relationship. And, in times of pain and turmoil, each person has his or her own resources to rely upon.

Relationships Are Created

You are mistaken if you believe that intimacy is merely a matter of "finding the right person." After you have found him or her, what happens next? Either a relationship will be **created** or it won't. When an intimate relationship develops, both people are actively involved every step of the way, beginning with the initial contact.

As is the case with any creative endeavor, you must be inner directed; that is, you must have a sense of where you are going and how you are going to get there. You must have a vision of what you are trying to create, as well as a realistic sense of what is required of you. Regardless of your experience in intimate relationships, your role-models or lack thereof, whether you come from a functional or dysfunctional family, there are specific strategies and skills that must be learned. **Anyone can learn them, and with the right partner, anyone can create an intimate relationship!**

A creative process is one of discovering as you go, learning as you gain experience. There will be times when you're dating that you will be at your best and still fall short. There will also be occasions when you will be subpar and something pleasantly surprising happens.

To be successful, you must be highly **motivated** and **committed** to creating quality relationships, and you must **believe in yourself.**

It is your **motivation** that keeps you actively involved in the creative process. It's passion, intensity and determination. There must be something you want, something that impels you to go after it and to keep going after it in the face of discouragement and disappointment. Often times, motivation comes from being in touch with the yearning for closeness and connection with another human being.

Commitment means following up your motivation with action, making a concerted effort, gaining the necessary experience and developing the skills that make intimacy possible. It means constantly practicing -- whenever the opportunity presents itself. It means paying attention to the communication process, particularly to your own tendencies: what you talk about and what you don't talk about, when you open up and when you close down, when you are listening and when you aren't listening, when you are being listened to and when you aren't. Being committed means becoming more aware of your feelings and reactions and incorporating them into your conversations. If you tend to be fearful and defensive, it will be necessary for you to learn to open up and trust.

You must also have the firm **belief** that you are capable of creating an intimate relationship and that as long as you keep at it, you will eventually be successful. When you find yourself frustrated with the people you meet and the kinds of experiences you are having, it is necessary to remember that with each experience, regardless of how disappointing it might be, you are moving closer to what you're trying to accomplish.

While it is a tremendous challenge to learn and grow from what are often frustrating and seemingly unproductive encounters, it helps to remember that they are part of a much larger process of creation, one in which you participate in order to make the connection that leads to an intimate relationship. Without such a perspective, you will be much more vulnerable to demoralization.

Gaining the Necessary Experience

How do you know whether you have what it takes to be in an intimate relationship? How do you prepare for one?

Dating can be viewed as "training" or "preparation" -- the first step in learning to sustain a long-term relationship.

Most people don't realize that **the processes and challenges involved in dating are the same as those involved in sustaining an intimate relationship.** In both cases, the process of communication is involved, and we must deal with negative feelings, conflicts and differences. In the context of dating, the objective is to generate rapport. In later stages of relationship, we're deepening the existing rapport.

The reality is, however, that while the processes and challenges may be the same, they become increasingly difficult the longer two people stay together. Contrary to what we might expect, the trials and tribulations involved in dating pale in comparison with those experienced in later stages of intimate relationships. The reasons for this are:

A) The "getting to know" process is generally more exciting than "knowing" each other and living together.

B) Usually, two people are initially drawn to each other because of what they like about each other and what they have in common. As time passes, the darker, more negative sides of one another come to light, as do differences.

C) Problems arise in the natural course of life that create stress in the relationship -- for example: career and financial problems, sickness, death, accidents, children, etc. The commitment two people have must be strong enough to withstand these stresses. They must also be able to communicate effectively enough to get through them.

If we learn to communicate effectively during our dating encounters, we should be able to do so once we are in a relationship, as well as be able to do so in any later stage of the relationship.

Is intimacy worth the risks and struggles we must face in order to achieve it?

There is simply no substitute for the sense of purpose and fulfillment that an intimate relationship provides. For me in my marriage, the sense of **knowing**, **trusting**, **accepting** and **respecting** each other on a deep level -- of being able to face problems and work together to solve them -- is one of great fortune and prosperity.

When such an experience is lacking, we're often aware that something essential is missing in our lives. Yet ironically, when we're in an intimate relationship, it is easy to take it for granted. Often times, it's not until you stop and look at how well you've gotten to know each other, at what you've accomplished in a partnership, at what you've been through and how long you've been together, that you are filled with appreciation and joy. Unquestionably, the feeling that you are not alone in your struggles, that another person is there doing his or her best to support and understand you -- and that you are there for him or her as well -- makes it all worthwhile.

· · CHAPTER TWO · ·

HAPPILY EVER NOW

What Is a Date?

A date is simply a time-limited encounter, the purpose of which is to assess whether you want a second date. You have a certain amount of time (I recommend a minimum of two hours) to focus and participate in the dating process; that is, to be with another person, get to know each other and see how you feel so you can decide whether you wish to pursue further contact.

After the first date, the decision is whether to have a second date. Either you will want to or you won't, or you'll have mixed feelings. If you've dated a person several times, the decision will be whether to continue to see him or her. If a relationship has materialized, the decision will be about defining the kind of relationship you wish to have -- whether you want to be friends or lovers or create something in between lovers and friends, or whether you no longer want to pursue it.

The idea is to be conscious of the fact that **at any time** during the course of a relationship you may want a change. Therefore, it is necessary at all times to be **prepared to discuss the direction you want the relationship to take!**

Healthy, creative dating involves: **assessment** (of your own feelings and needs), **communication** (about feelings toward each other and the relationship), **decision** and **action** taken, all of which are done in the "**here and now.**"

Being in the Moment

In order to be in the moment, in the "here and now," a perspective of time -- both in the long-term and short-term sense -- is essential. When we stop and look at the quality of our lives -- of all the time spent -- what we have is a composite of the substance and quality of all those moments. Yet, because our experience of time is moment by moment, the more present and alive we are in each moment, the richer and more meaningful our lives will be. Therefore, whenever you are with someone, what truly matters is what's happening at that time, not what has happened in the past or what will happen in the future.

As time passes and you look back on experiences you've had, their significance and meaning change. We tend to make more out of them at the time they occurred than we do when recalling them at some later date. Some things stand out, and many things are completely forgotten.

Your memory serves as a reminder of the passage of time, of your growth and of lessons learned. Do you remember your first date? Your first boyfriend or girlfriend? The first year of a significant relationship? The fifth year? The tenth? Most likely, what you felt then is different from what you feel now. How you handled situations then is often not the way you would handle them now. You change! The way you feel and act at any given time depends on the various circumstances existing at that time, and these are constantly changing.

The understanding that you are changing all the time can be freeing. When you know that whatever is happening is happening "here and now," you have a way of framing your experience, a context. This makes it easier to accept and express your feelings, whether positive or negative, regardless of how another person responds to you.

A short- and long-term perspective on how relationships evolve is also essential. In the long-term scheme of things, one meeting is relatively insignificant. No matter how great any one date may be, no matter how attracted you are to each other or how comfortable you feel, it's only one date, and relationships aren't made in one date. For instance, there's no guarantee the two of you will feel or relate the same way in subsequent encounters. In dating, therefore, it is important to "cross each bridge when you get to it," and not before. If your attention is on what will or might happen, you will miss the essence of what is happening. (A common pitfall is projecting into the future and assuming there is more of a relationship than there actually is, which usually ends up becoming a painful experience.)

Even though in the long-term scheme of things one date may seem insignificant, in the short-term scheme of things, relationships actually develop **one date at a time**. The level of intimacy achieved during each and every contact determines the overall quality of the relationship. Therefore, in order to maximize your chance for a quality relationship, it is necessary to be fully involved in the present and make the most out of each and every encounter.

Great Expectations

Many of us carry around an inaccurate and unrealistic concept of what is supposed to happen on a date. In the midst of the usual excitement and fears associated with dating, our tendency is to either inflate or deflate the significance of one date. If we do this (inflate or deflate) it is likely that we will not be emotionally prepared for the realities of dating or intimate relationships.

For example, you might begin a date looking for your "dream person," "that perfect somebody," the person you will marry, a person to be the father or mother of your children. If you like the person, you'll tend to think in these futuristic terms and act as if your whole future will be decided by this one date. This makes it appear there is much more at stake than there actually is. You'll lose sight of the fact that no matter how great or terrible any one date is, relationships are built one date at a time. Looking beyond the next date into the future often creates so much anxiety you can no longer be spontaneous. This will ultimately take the fun out of dating.

On the other hand, you don't want to deflate the significance of any one date. Unrealistic expectations, a history of poor relationships and a string of disappointing dating experiences cause many of us to deflate the significance of a date. Thoughts like, "What's the use? Nothing worthwhile will come out of it" can obscure the process and purpose of dating. These thoughts often become self-fulfilling prophecies. When we lose motivation, we stop being creative and we stop learning. If we can remember that all we are trying to do is get a feeling for whether we want to get together a second time -- and that either we will or we won't -- it will be easier to stay focused and not get discouraged by any one experience.

The attitude, "If it's not love at first sight, then why bother?" is another example. It sets us up for disappointment and deflation. Remember, love doesn't just happen! In order to create and maintain a relationship, we must work hard at it. We must often deal with negative feelings, conflicts and differences. There's no other way. When there is an agenda to "fall in love," chances are you will overlook the simple task in front of you -- to get to know the other person enough to decide whether you want to see him or her for a second date. You will look for qualities in the other person you wish him or her to possess, while overlooking the qualities he or she is presenting to you at the moment. You may try to look good and act your best, rather than be relaxed and spontaneous.

The Best and Worst That Can Happen

To come to a date prepared to participate fully, it's necessary to maintain a realistic perspective about the best and worst that can happen.

There are four possible outcomes to every date:

1) You'll want to see the person again, and the feeling will be mutual.

2) You'll want to get together again, but the other person won't.

3) The other person will want to get together again, but you won't.

4) You won't want to see him or her again, and the feeling will be mutual.

Bear in mind that you will face these outcomes every time you date and that, like it or not, the odds of an intimate relationship developing are not good. Most of the time, for one reason or another, you will not want to see the person again.

Because there is no way to control the natural course of events, it's futile to try. Rather than getting caught up in a never-ending cycle of highs and lows, **enter into a date prepared to deal with any outcome!** Each outcome poses a different emotional challenge.

In the first outcome both of you are interested and attracted and want to see each other again. As many of us may well know, this outcome is the most preferred, yet many people get themselves into trouble. The tendency is to project into the future, to assume the person is "right" for you and that a wonderful relationship is in the making. Rather than dealing with the concept of a second date, we're thinking about where to spend the night. The last thing on our minds is that it's only one date, that relationships develop one date at time and that we might not feel and act the same way the next time we are together. The challenge is to not get too involved too soon.

On the other end of the spectrum is the fear that the second date will not be as good as the first. Even though a mutual attraction and desire to get together again is what most of us wish for when we date, it doesn't mean we'll express these feelings. This situation often brings up a variety of fears related to not getting what we want or to being let down, so the more excited we are, the more insecure we feel. When we are feeling insecure, a common tendency is to take a self-protective stance that invariably inhibits communication. We won't take the risk of saying that we are attracted or want to get together again, which leaves us wondering what might have happened "had I taken the risk." When it's only a second date at stake, we will tend to be less excited, therefore less insecure, more inclined to communicate and more inclined to get together again.

For example, when they dated, both Jessica and Andrew had fears about getting together again:

Andrew: I really enjoyed the evening with you. I am attracted to you and definitely would like to see you again. But I'm afraid when I see you again, the novelty will have worn off, which has happened to me before -- more than once.

Jessica: I'm afraid you won't like me as much and won't want to see me again. I'm fantasizing about what if we go out and have fun together...I immediately take it to sex, without knowing the person well enough. I don't have much experience being with someone just to be with him.

Jessica and Andrew's discussion allowed them to focus on the "here and now." It made them less concerned about what had happened in the past and what might happen in the future. They felt freer to go ahead and take the risk of getting together again.

In the second situation, when you are attracted or interested but the other person isn't, the challenge is dealing with rejection. Granted, rejection never feels good. But the question is, how bad will you feel? Is your self-esteem wrapped up with how someone you've spent a few hours with -- someone you don't know -- responds to you? This is one of the great pitfalls of dating.

For example, this is what happened when Teresa expressed interest in Wil. After pleasantries about how great a time they had together (but never broaching the subject of a second date), Teresa finally mustered the courage to tell Wil she'd like to see him again.

At that point, things got tense. Wil stood there silent and paralyzed. Teresa's mood changed from eagerness to feeling like she had done something wrong.

Wil eventually gathered himself and said, "Well, I suppose that's possible."

Teresa asked him what the problem was. "I guess I feel put on the spot, that an expectation is placed on me."

Exasperated, Teresa replied, "All I said was that I'd like to see you again. I'm not asking you to have my baby!"

In the ensuing discussion, several things came to light. Wil admitted he had not really taken the date seriously and had merely gone through the motions, as he had so many times before. He explained that his pattern had been to silently decide to not see the woman again. Once he'd made that decision, he would then try and get through the date with as little discomfort as possible.

Wil also revealed that Teresa's expression of interest had made him feel guilty: "It brought up my fears about commitment. I guess I got hung up about whether this could be a long-term relationship or not." His criterion for rejecting Teresa was "a kind of superficial thing. Like when my eyes met yours, sparks didn't fly."

Teresa's reacted: "Jesus Christ! I'm not asking you to have my baby. It's just a second date!..." She was fed up. "This is what always happens. I put myself out and then I get rejected. I can't say how many times this has happened to me. And it just happened again."

Was Teresa better off keeping her feelings to herself and not risk the pain of rejection (again)? What if anything short of interest on Wil's part triggered a whole array of painful feelings that weren't necessarily related to him? Should her willingness to risk in the future hinge on his acceptance or rejection of her?

Teresa's difficulty handling Wil's rejection had to do with her communication being **conditional** -- there was an expectation or need for her interest to be reciprocated.

When your communication is conditional, its existence is in the hands of the other person. No one should have the power to take this away from you. When at the core of your interest is the desire to create an intimate relationship, your interest is internally based and should remain constant regardless of what happens externally.

In the third situation -- when you are not interested, but the other person is interested in you -- feelings of guilt are commonly triggered. No one likes to be in the position of hurting another person's feelings. What often happens is that we don't say how we really feel. We don't say, "No, I don't want to pursue it" or, "I'm not interested." Instead we say things like, "We could get together again as friends." A lot of times we wind up continuing to see that person. Or we say that we had a good time but never contact that person again.

For instance, when Tony dated Meritt, he had tremendous difficulty telling Meritt clearly he wasn't interested in pursuing a relationship. He was unaccustomed to coming right out and saying how he felt, especially when it came to negative feelings.

Even though Tony had no desire to see Meritt again, instead of addressing his feelings regarding a second date and finding out about hers, he told her he "wanted to be friends."

What did he mean, "friends"?

His reply: "I didn't want to leave with her feeling badly towards me. I try to have harmonious relationships with every person I meet. Who knows? Maybe we'd be able to do business together at some point in the future."

Meritt was confused and somewhat dismayed. "Given how far apart we were, it's unlikely that we'd become friends, let alone, maintain a friendship. Besides, I don't want to foster a friendship with every person I meet."

Tony entered into his date with Meritt with at least one ulterior motive, perhaps two. He needed to be liked by every woman regardless of how he felt toward her, and he wanted to develop business contacts. By trying to make every date have a "happy ending," he was going against the forces of reality and nature. His motivation to "stay friends" or "to do business together in the future" had more to do with his unconscious need to escape the difficult feelings of being with someone he didn't wish to see again (and who didn't want to see him again) than with any genuine desire to develop a friendship. He also believed that any of the less desirable dating outcomes would somehow reap undesirable consequences. As long as he believed this and behaved accordingly, it was impossible for him to deal with his feelings in the moment.

When you resort to the term "friend" to avoid dealing with negative feelings, you are diminishing the concept of friendship and thereby doing yourself a disservice. When you call someone who isn't a friend a friend, you've lost sight of what a friend really is. A friend is an intimate partner; if you can't be friends, you can't be intimate, and if you can't be intimate, you can't be friends. Friendship is generally as special and significant a relationship as any could be. If we are to live fulfilling lives, friends are vital. It's not a term that should be used loosely or to escape uncomfortable feelings.

The fourth situation -- when the date is a bust all the way around -- is relief compared with situations two and three. When the date is a complete fiasco -- no interest, no chemistry, you can't wait for it to be over -- the challenge is to not get too discouraged, but rather get to motivated for another date with someone else.

Let's use the analogy of playing baseball. It's a long season and every game is important. A great game or a terrible one, what difference does it make? The best players maintain the highest level of play possible for the duration of the season -- the highest batting average. Regardless of whether they hit three home runs or strike out three times in a game, there is always the next game. They're not worried about the previous game. They don't play "scared." Worse than a bad game is the feeling that they did not play the best they could.

The same goes for dating. The "highest level of play" is being real, expressing how you feel, seeking the same from your partner and doing so on a consistent basis.

"Dating Partnership"

Given that you want to be able to effectively handle any dating situation, it might help to establish a mutual understanding at the beginning of a date about what the purpose of the encounter is. Call it entering into a time-limited "**dating partnership**" or a "**dating contract.**"

Once it is mutually agreed that both parties are "checking each other out" and will, at the end, **discuss** and **decide** about further contact, it should be easier to date without any obligation to make it anything other than what it is.

We can call the process of discussing and deciding **bringing the date to closure**.

While establishing "partnership" and "bringing the date to closure" may seem contrived or artificial to some people, the idea is for you to enter into the date clear about the parameters and purpose for being together. This includes how much time you want to spend together and talking about future contact before parting ways.

I recommend that you make the "contract" and "closure" part of the dating ritual. There are a number of advantages in doing so. You will:

1) Have many more opportunities to practice and develop your communication skills.

2) Open the doors of communication, creating an opportunity to learn more about each other. The process of dis-

cussing how you truly feel makes it possible for you to receive feedback about how you came across **and** for you to better understand your partner's feelings and behavior.

3) Expend less energy wondering what your partner is feeling because you will both be on the same wavelength, having established common purposes for meeting and agreed on the amount of time you'll spend as well as honestly discussed plans for a second date. The unspoken "contract" is to be temporary partners in play and agree that both people will be "**good sports and will survive any outcome!**" As a result of this contract, you will be able to proceed more freely and have more peace of mind.

4) Build self-esteem: behavior that is aligned with your purpose is self-affirming. As long as you've been honest, which is an end in itself, you'll feel like you accomplished what you set out to do. You will feel like you made constructive use of your time and that you did the best you could. Regardless of the outcome, you'll feel better about yourself. Conversely, if you are not honest -- for instance saying "yes" when you mean "no" or calling someone who isn't a friend a friend -- chances are you will not walk away feeling good about yourself.

5) Gain experience in taking responsibility for creating the quality of relationship you're seeking. Taking responsibility -- making decisions -- is part of life.

Prepare for the Future, Handle the Moment

Dating is an opportunity to gain experience telling the truth about how you feel at any given time.

If you take the risk and say which direction you'd like the relationship to go and a relationship does materialize, it is much more likely that it will be a healthy one, characterized by openness, honesty and understanding. If you do but a relationship does not materialize, you will have moved toward achieving a standard of relating necessary to create and sustain intimate relationships. If you don't and a relationship doesn't develop, you've probably blown an opportunity to discover something new about yourself, the other person or the relationship. If you don't and a relationship evolves, chances are greater that its foundation will not be one that lends itself to conflict-resolution and mutual understanding.

· · CHAPTER THREE · ·

"THE WRITING IS ON THE WALL"

Relationships begin on the first date, and they continue from where they begin. The way they start is the way they continue. The stage for a healthy or unhealthy relationship is set during the initial encounter. The interactive patterns two people establish the first time they are together can be likened to a replicating DNA molecule; that is, they continue in subsequent encounters. In this way, the first date is a microcosm of the entire relationship.

Communication is a "cause and effect" process. If what you communicate is not representative of what is natural and true for you, it's likely the responses you elicit from your partner won't be representative of what is natural and true for him or her as well. Defensiveness and dishonesty breed defensiveness and dishonesty. Conversely, openness and honesty breed openness and honesty.

Misconceptions

A common misconception is that we need not open up and "be real" on a first date because **it doesn't count** unless there is a second date or until an actual relationship exists. Many people, for example, say to the person they're with that they had fun or that they would like to be friends without having any intention of getting together again. Their behavior is based on the idea that if they do not intend to get together again, it is okay to misrepresent the truth. They are, in effect, telling themselves that if the date doesn't go the way they want it to, the way they behave is completely inconsequential, as if nothing ever took place.

Every contact, every exchange, every hour and minute we are in communication counts. Each and every encounter is a relationship in itself. This relationship may not go beyond a single encounter, or it may evolve into a lasting one. Whenever two people communicate they are simultaneously in a relationship and are in the process of creating one. Therefore, regardless of whether we are with someone one time or several times, it is necessary to establish healthy and consistent behavior patterns.

Another common misconception is that it isn't necessary to be open and honest during a first date because **it's easier to do so later,** "after we've gotten to know each other better" or "after we've established trust." Often times, if the willingness is not there from the start, we do not get a second chance. Moreover, if we are not open on the first date and we continue seeing that person, we will not be more inclined to open up.

Actually, **it is easier to be honest the first time you're with someone than any time thereafter.** The more contact we have with someone, the greater investment of time and energy we've made. If we care about a person, we invest ourselves emotionally. The more invested we are, the greater the risk of being hurt or losing what we have. The fear of being hurt is, in turn, a precursor of self-protection. Defensive, self-protective postures conflict with our natural ability to be interested, honest and empathetic in relationships. And when, as a result of our history in relationships, we enter into encounters anticipating getting hurt and lacking faith that a relationship can endure, we are that much more defensive.

When you consider the multitude of uncomfortable, negative and painful situations that all couples must contend with at one time or another, you might have doubts about whether you are even up to the challenge. But if you set a precedent for open and honest communication the first time you meet someone, before you start to really care about each other, it will be easier to build on what has already been started than to change an existing pattern. People generally do not change their style of relating midway in a relationship. For example, if you are accustomed to expressing your true feelings, you don't suddenly shut down or try to conceal them. If you're accustomed to not saying what you're truly feeling, you don't suddenly open up, unless there are extenuating circumstances that cause you to do so, such as a betrayal or therapeutic intervention.

Conflict Has Its Place

If two people resolve a conflict and achieve understanding about their differences the first time they're together, it is more likely that they will be able to continue to do so in subsequent interactions.

My first date with my wife Barbara is a case in point. We got caught up in a highly emotionally charged conflict that was either going to get resolved or put an end to future contact.

Both of us were unaware we had entered into the date with different assumptions about who was going to pay. I had expected her to pay for herself. She expected me to pay for her. We were in for a rude awakening.

I had asked Barbara to meet me for dinner. That night we spent several hours in a Chinese restaurant, talking and laughing. It felt great to be with her because we were able to share so much about ourselves. I was so appreciative of her company that when it came time to leave I said, "I'm having such a good time with you, I think I'll pay for dinner."

All of a sudden Barbara's mood changed. Although she was smiling, I detected hostility as she said, "What do you mean, you're having such a good time that you'll pay? After all, you invited me out to dinner, didn't you?" I said, "I invited you out for dinner as I would any friend. I wanted to share your company. I was not thinking of taking you out. Asking women out doesn't mean that I automatically pay for them!"

Barbara was outraged. "Some things you should just know," she said. "You extended an invitation to me and therefore should pay without question." Again, she reiterated, "You asked me out!"

I got more upset. "Why should I treat you to dinner? Didn't you want to have dinner with me? After all, I didn't ask you if you wanted me to pay your way! Where did you get the idea I should?" Barbara hesitated to respond at first. Eventually however, she mustered the courage to explain her point of view: "I just really love to be taken out. It makes me feel special, and I enjoy feeling special when I'm on a date."

I understood what Barbara was saying, but I still felt taken for granted. I said, "But what about me? Doesn't what I want matter, too?" I added, with a measure of sarcasm, "Maybe all you really want to know about me is what you can get without having to ask me."

Fortunately, she didn't react to my sarcasm, and she seemed to hear that I was upset by having expectations placed on me and that I felt she hadn't acknowledged my show of appreciation. She opened up a bit more. "I do care about what you want," she said. "It just makes me feel good to be treated sometimes."

Then a light went on in my head. I understood what Barbara was saying. Her comments were not a personal affront to me. She was merely telling me that she didn't get the chance to feel special very often.

I also realized that my outrage toward Barbara had more to do with my personal, lifelong struggle to define myself as an individual than with her expectation that I treat her. How could she possibly have known that I had been rebelling against convention all my life by defying every norm? She was taught that "the man pays for dinner," and whenever she had gone on a date, the man did pay for dinner, so there was no reason for her to think otherwise. I had no right to dump on her.

However, it is not at all unusual to react negatively to something a person says or does when it wasn't intended that way, especially in dating situations in which people are meeting for the first time. When I offered to pay, I expected Barbara to receive my offer as I intended it, as an expression of appreciation and acknowledgment. I was taken completely by surprise, and so was she.

This first date was challenging to both of us. Because the issue of who should pay was a volatile one, it was easy to get sidetracked. If either of us had been concerned with presenting ourselves as people who know how to behave "correctly," who never argue, and if we had concealed our true feelings, we would not have gotten past our appearances.

By taking the risk that our honesty might alienate the other and that we might be "wrong," we discovered that we were able to express feelings of resentment, anger, hurt and fear, and this is what a lasting, intimate relationship is founded on. We established then and there that when "push comes to shove," we were solid enough within ourselves to face negativity, conflict and differences, and we were looking for someone who could do the same.

This was the first time I experienced what I would call a "deeper" intimacy -- one characterized by ability to communicate and by knowing, trusting, accepting and respecting each other. At some point, before the end of four hours, a fight and a reconciliation, I found myself in pursuit of a friend, and so did she. It was as if we both decided at the same time to make a commitment. There was no doubt about it, we both felt "great chemistry" -- sexual, emotional and spiritual.

The ultimate significance of this initial conflict cannot be overstated. Through it, Barbara and I learned that we were able to get past our differences and uncomfortable feelings to achieve a mutual understanding. I told her how things were for me. She told me how they were for her. As a result, we both felt closer and more respectful of each other and wanted to continue seeing each other. In our case, the "writing was on the wall." Our ability to achieve mutual understanding continued in subsequent encounters.

Avoid Now, Pay Later

When the inability to achieve understanding characterizes an initial encounter, it's likely that this difficulty will show up again and again throughout the course of the developing relationship. Therefore, the time to express how you really feel with someone is during the first encounter.

An example of how not revealing one's true feelings can create problems later in a relationship occurred during Maureen and Tony's date.

Toward the end of their date, Tony approached Maureen with the intention of giving her a hug. Even though she felt uncomfortable, she did not say anything and allowed him to hug her anyway.

Maureen wasn't sure how to interpret this gesture, nor did she understand what it meant to Tony. She wondered, "Does he think I'm going to go to bed with him?" but she never asked him what was on his mind. Her discomfort had to do with associating such demonstrations of affection with a later stage of relationship, but she didn't discuss her feelings with him. One of her reasons for not saying anything was, "I was wondering what's wrong with me for not wanting a hug?"

When I asked Maureen what would have happened if she and Tony continued to date and Tony continued to hug her without her permission, Maureen said, "I'd probably be angry and think that he was some kind of jerk, that he was taking advantage of me. I'd think that he didn't pick up on my feelings and, therefore, didn't care about me. I wouldn't want to do anything for him. I'd be on his case."

Apparent in Maureen's response was a pattern. She was counting on men to read her mind. This way, she wouldn't have to deal with her discomfort and resentment directly and openly. As long as the man could understand her desires, needs and feelings without her having to make them known to him, she felt great about him. But when he didn't respond in a way that displayed the requisite understanding, she'd blame him. She wasn't taking responsibility for her own behavior. In her mind, whatever transpired was her date's responsibility.

Had a relationship between Maureen and Tony materialized, Maureen would have built up so much anger that she would have become extremely critical and hostile toward Tony. Tony would have had no idea what was provoking such assaulting behavior. Chances are the relationship would have dissipated in mutual recrimination and frustration.

If Maureen had told Tony how she felt about his hugging her, the developing relationship would have taken a different direction. At the point at which she became aware of her discomfort, all she had to say was something like, "I'm a bit uncomfortable with you hugging me right now and would prefer that you don't." (No further explanation would have been necessary.) If he had reacted defensively or couldn't understand her, she would have found out that he wasn't a suitable partner. On the other hand, if he responded with understanding, they would have had a more solid foundation to build on. She would have had the experience of being vulnerable, of taking a risk and of achieving understanding. She would have felt better about herself and Tony as a result.

The "Ninety-nine Percent" Phenomenon

I was recently challenged on the premise that relationships begin on the first date.

"The relationship that comes to my mind doesn't fit at all. I was with her for a year before any serious problems presented themselves. I liked ninety-nine percent of the person. It was during the course of the second year that I started feeling I disliked ninety-nine percent. I had no idea we'd have so much conflict and be so unable to resolve it. She wasn't who I thought she was. The relationship became intolerable, but it took a whole year before the flip-flop occurred."

Good point! Maybe I should slightly modify the principle to read as follows: **Relationships begin after your first fight!** It's not until two people have a major conflict that they discover how intimate they actually are. If your first date (and all subsequent dates for that matter) is devoid of conflict, differences and negative feelings and there aren't any problems that must be resolved, this is not by any means an indication that your relationship (if one materializes) will be forever free of conflict and pain!

In the situation described above, it is likely that this couple wasn't in touch with their feelings, tried to avoid the negative ones or placed too much emphasis on romance or on sex. It's possible that due to lack of experience and communication skills, they remained stuck in the early (easier) stages of relationship; that is they based their relationship solely on what they liked and had in common and avoided everything else. If this was the case, it's not too surprising that it took a year to find out they were incompatible.

Exercise: The Writing on the Wall

Recall how one of your significant relationships began. What happened that caused you to develop a relationship?

If the relationship ended, did the issues and dynamics causing its demise exist the first time you were together? If so, were you overlooking or denying them?

If the relationship is still intact, were the factors contributing to its success operating at the time you first met?

·· CHAPTER FOUR ··

THE "CLEAN SLATE"

Each and every initial encounter should be a "**clean slate**," the end of what was and the beginning of something new.

The "clean slate" concept can be looked upon as a state of mind characterized by openness and spontaneity. Call it the "Zen of dating." It means entering into an encounter in the spirit of discovery, not knowing what is going to happen. A first date may be thought of as a new play about to unfold, one that has never been acted before. It is an improvisation in which two people are creating the dialogue and drama right then and there.

Obviously, when two people meet for the first time, they have no history together. Because they don't know each other and have little invested, the fear of rejection should be at its lowest. One would hope that during an initial encounter, openness and spontaneity occur naturally and effortlessly.

I've come to recognize, unfortunately, that in the majority of initial encounters, the relationship stage has already been set and the dialogue scripted before the participants have even met. Most dates are doomed before they even begin.

Emotional Baggage From Prior Relationships

The principal source of counterproductive behavior in dating and relationships is the residue from whatever emotional trauma we have suffered in prior relationships. Most people have learned to mistrust others and mobilize their defenses in order to stop feeling and protect themselves from getting hurt. They haven't had the experience of safety. What they have in fact experienced is that expressing their feelings posed a threat to their well-being throughout the course of their lives. Their behavior is based on the premise that "**if I let you get to know me, you'll hurt me.**" This defensive posture, while understandable, makes it impossible for anyone to really get to know them and for them to get to know others.

When this is the case, we enter new situations as if we have been there before. We act as if we know only one way of behaving and can't adapt to new situations or people. There is no distinguishing previous relationships from present ones. The present and future become reenactments of the past.

It's amazing to realize the extent to which many people habitually react to individuals they do not know as if they were their mothers or fathers. "He's just like my father" and "she's just like my mother" are common complaints. When we jump to these types of conclusions, the ability to discover what the other person is really like vanishes. He may be just like your father, and he may not be. The point is, you'll never find out! Rarely does the idea of telling someone that "you remind me of my father (or mother)" enter our minds.

The concepts "clean slate," a "new start" or "another chance" can give hope to those who wish there was some way to leave the past behind. In dating, there is no past, only the present. There's no reason to anticipate rejection, abandonment, betrayal or any other feared experience. The future hasn't happened, and until it does, it's nothing more than a fear or projection.

When two people are discovering each other, they have a chance to act in new ways. Because it is the **first and only time** you've been with this person, you may assume more trust than you otherwise would. You may proceed as if your trust had never been broken. It is an ideal time to experiment with new behaviors, especially when the old ones haven't worked. For example, you may say things you don't ordinarily say or not say the things you usually do. You can try opening up and expressing your feelings with the faith that you won't suffer the same negative consequences you have in the past. If you get hurt, the hurt should be in proportion to the experience of being rejected one time from someone who doesn't know you. The fact that this is the first and only time should minimize the damage. Even if the other person's response to your honesty does resemble a prior hurtful experience, you may find that you feel differently about this experience in the present and that you have other options.

Rejected Once Again

When Mary arrived twenty minutes late to meet Joe, he reacted as if she was like all the other women in his life -- unreliable and rejecting. He automatically assumed that she wasn't going to show up at all.

When Mary finally arrived, Joe was seething. Rather than immediately finding out why she was late, he treated her coldly. She didn't understand his behavior and, in turn, felt mistrustful. They had no chance to achieve an understanding about the feelings that were evoked in him or about the circumstances surrounding her lateness. Their date was ruined before it began.

Clearly for Joe, their first date was not a "clean slate." He had entered this encounter with the belief and expectation that he would be rejected. His experience became a self-fulfilling prophecy.

When this happened, Joe was incapable of seeing the situation for what it was -- a date with a woman he had never been with before. Yes, she was late, and how many of us enjoy waiting and wondering if our date is going to show up? But this was the first time this had happened with Mary. Joe didn't have any idea why she was late.

Granted, we are often unaware when we overreact or don't understand why. But the question we must ask ourselves is: "Are we **capable** of regulating the degree of hurt and subsequent defensiveness?" I believe the answer is "yes." Being able to distinguish the past from the present -- remembering that our dates are "never before" events -- helps. With this awareness, a whole wellspring of hurt doesn't have to be triggered or acted upon.

Joe could have responded with something like, "What happened?" or "I'm upset you're late." This would have given Mary a chance to explain and apologize, at which time Joe's anger probably would have turned into understanding. The fact that she was late would no longer have been an issue.

"No One's Really Interested"

When Kate went out with Brian, she liked him. However, she thought she talked a lot, that she took up Brian's time and that he was just being polite by not saying anything. She could not bring herself to let him know that she really enjoyed being with him, nor was she able to ask him whether he was enjoying her company. Rather than dealing with her feelings, she tried to "talk her anxieties away."

Kate had not begun the date with a clean slate. Instead, she embarked upon her first date with Brian with the assumption that, like others before, he did not really want to be with her. Clearly, her underlying belief originated at a different time with different people. Her fear made her summon her defenses against being herself and acting spontaneously, thus effectively extinguishing any chance she had to discover that she could be wrong. She reacted as if she was the child and Brian was the father who never acknowledged her.

When we are behaving in a way that is consistent with a "clean slate," nothing is predetermined. We are in the present. We do this by "reality-checking" our reactions, by incorporating the thoughts and feelings that get triggered into the conversation. Unless we create a contrasting experience for ourselves, we will not be in a position to see whether the emotional baggage we carry around with us -- our underlying beliefs, expectations and reactions -- still apply.

Preconceived Notions

Our preconceived notions about what is supposed to happen on a date, the kind of person we're looking for and what our relationships should be like also contaminate the "clean slate."

Preconceived notions are mostly idealized images and stereotypes. Some of these images are handed down to us from our parents. Many of them have filtered into our brains after years of watching television and movies or reading newspapers and books.

The primary problem with preconceived notions is that we are usually unaware of harboring them. Therefore, we do not realize the extent to which we use the dating process in an attempt to convert fantasy into reality. When the reality doesn't fit our romantic vision (which it rarely does) we are disappointed. More importantly, when we try to match unreal images with real people and experiences, we set up obstacles that prevent the initial dating interaction from unfolding naturally. Because we do not respond spontaneously and in the moment, but according to the pictures in our heads, we effectively insulate ourselves from the person we are with and are supposed to be trying to get to know.

For example, Jim always associated New Year's Eve with a Champagne toast and kissing his date when the clock struck midnight. So, when he and Louise had their first date on New Year's Eve, he chose a place where he could order Champagne and watch the clock. Jim made sure that he and Louise were at the bar by midnight with the glasses in their hands ready to toast. Right on schedule, when the clock struck twelve, he leaned over to kiss Louise on the lips. Louise was taken aback by his presumptuousness and sudden intrusiveness. Clearly, she did not share Jim's preconceived notion of the perfect New Year's Eve. Not surprisingly, Jim felt let down because she had not wanted to celebrate New Year's Eve with him. How different Jim and Louise's date might have turned out had he opted to let it happen, rather than try to make it happen in a predetermined way.

Another example of how our preconceived notions can limit our opportunities to develop rapport with the people we date was reflected in a comment a client, Claire, made:

> "I only want to go out with Jewish men. I can't see myself with anyone who's not Jewish. In terms of really getting serious about someone, I want a man with whom I could feel at home and celebrate the holidays."

It wasn't Claire's preference for Jewish men that was limiting. It was her deciding prematurely which men were suitable ("only Jewish men...") before actually meeting and spending time with them that kept her from finding the best mate. She had made a decision based not on experience, but on faulty premises.

Claire's "sight unseen" selection process was antithetical to **discovering** what two people can create together. She assumed that whether a man was Jewish would ultimately determine whether she would be happy in a relationship with him. She was also adamant in her belief that for a man to appreciate and understand her cultural heritage, he would have to be Jewish.

Many of us make up rules about which types of people are suitable for us without ever allowing ourselves the experience that would tell us whether we are accurate in our projections. What if we're wrong? What if there are as many people who don't share our cultural background, yet can still appreciate it and us, as there are people who do share it and can appreciate us? None of these people would ever be given a chance. More importantly, sharing a common religion or any other categorical requirement -- be it race, socioeconomic class, age, physical size or attribute, occupation, etc. -- **in no way guarantees that warmth and understanding will follow.** On the other hand, when the qualities of openness, honesty and understanding are present, chances are we will be happier, more appreciated and more comfortable regardless of whether any predetermined criteria are met.

Claire reacted strongly to my point of view. "I'm fighting you because I don't agree. I don't want to be open to a man who is not Jewish. I don't think that a non-Jew could really understand me. I just can't let all that go."

Being open means being vulnerable, not in control, not knowing what is going to happen. Part of Claire's aversion to being open had to do with being with someone she doesn't know, which is a fairly common occurrence. Dating, by its very nature, is not a comfortable situation. The element of discovery, of surprise, is always lurking, and this conflicts with our need to feel safe and in control. The reality is that at any time, someone could walk into our lives, and we could have a profound connection with him or her. If we are trying to escape our discomfort by adhering to rules that preclude our experience, the possibility of being pleasantly surprised will be eliminated.

During our discussion, Claire began to understand the forces underlying her preconceived notions and how they had restricted her:

"I've been unwilling to go for a cup of coffee with a guy unless I consider him to be 'marriage material'! For long periods in my life, I've been disconnected from myself and have felt really distant and isolated from people. I used to use Judaism as a way to make a connection. It felt safe. But it was like a false sense of closeness and security. I've hung on to that for years. Whenever I'm with someone I know is Jewish, I automatically feel so much more comfortable. There is something really scary for me about being with someone I perceive as being very different. When I'm with people who aren't Jewish, it's like I'm not 'at home.' And that's what I've been told all my life:

that people who aren't Jewish are different. But if they are Jewish, they're supposed to be like family. And I've always assumed that this meant I could trust the person."

Based on the messages Claire received during her upbringing, she learned to associate being Jewish with sameness, familiarity and trustworthiness. Not being Jewish meant that the other person wasn't like her -- as if he was from a distant planet and was, therefore, unsafe to be with.

Claire continued:

> "Sometimes when I am attracted to someone who is not Jewish, I try to make them Jewish in my mind. Believing that **anybody** is a possible partner for me is way too scary, too alien. To think about sharing a home with someone not from my culture feels weird.
>
> "Up until recently, my point of connection with a man had always been sexual. I looked at men as potential bed partners. After years of 'one night stands,' and waking up with men I wanted to have nothing to do with, I learned that having sex isn't the way to find the man who is right for me.
>
> "So, in order to keep my sanity, I'd just made a blanket decision that certain people would be 'off limits.' I had decided not to be open with any person with whom I couldn't imagine living or being married to."

Claire learned to rely on what other people told her rather than her own feelings. It is understandable then, that Claire would have difficulty relating to the idea of maintaining an open mind, of approaching each date as a "clean slate" and assessing her various dating partners according to how she feels when she is with them. Her rule that prospective partners must be Jewish served to compensate for underdeveloped communication skills as well as a lack of confidence in her partner selection process. Rather than approaching dating as an opportunity to get to know each other, she thought she could skip this step altogether and have knowing each other, building trust, etc., depend on whether someone is Jewish (or by having sex).

Claire is an example of how we can delude ourselves in order to feel safe in situations in which there is no safety to be had. Because we don't really know anything about our dating partners or how the date will unfold, it is necessary to maintain an open mind, yet also be prepared for surprises, pleasant and unpleasant. There is no way of judging relationship suitability without first experiencing the person. We'd like to believe that when certain qualifications are met, such as religion, age, occupation, attractiveness, an intimate relationship is in the making. The fact is, one may or may not be. If a relationship does materialize, the intimacy achieved during any one date will most likely be the result of mutual open-mindedness and ability to communicate.

As Claire gets more in touch with her feelings, she will eventually be able to rely on them as vital sources of information. She will likely become more open-minded, take more risks and learn more from her dating experiences. Her criteria for judging character and compatibility will be based more on her experience with each individual than on preconceived notions or idealized images. By paying more attention to how she feels, she will **discover** the extent to which her dating partners exude the warmth and understanding she is looking for. The types of men she will be drawn to and the ones she gets involved with, will, no doubt, change.

This discussion raises the question "Why are the 'wrong' people always chasing me while the 'right' ones are nowhere to be found?" Part of the answer has to do with a pattern of arbitrarily rejecting people who don't fit our pictures and pursuing only those who do. And part of the answer has to do with how we compensate for not knowing how to decide whether someone is right for us.

While a common cultural background is an important consideration in dating, it shouldn't be the sole or primary one.

The question being raised here is, "What are the grounds for a lasting, intimate relationship?" Common cultural backgrounds are certainly a factor, but how big a factor? It varies. For some people, coming from totally different cultures simplifies the communication process, and for some people, sharing a cultural heritage makes communication more difficult. Sometimes sharing the same cultural heritage helps tremendously, and sometimes different backgrounds doom relationships.

But some things we do know. Regardless of whether two people share a cultural heritage, there will be negative feelings, conflicts and differences in any relationship. The individuals involved and their ability to communicate are overriding factors. If they are able to talk to each other about what they want and need in a relationship, there is hope. Through communication, they will find out whether they are well suited.

I know from my own experience how far from reality preconceived notions can be. I was dead-set about Jewish women, as if I had met every Jewish woman in the world, as if I'd respond the same way to each women. There was a time when I swore that I wouldn't date or marry a Jewish woman. I harbored a lot of judgments about Jewish women. I saw them as materialistic, superficial, overly critical and domineering. Jewish women and I were like oil and water. I believed that the only women who could really understand and appreciate me, who were emotionally accessible, and with whom I could get along, were non-Jews. In the three significant relationships I had with non-Jewish women, my experiences confirmed my beliefs. Our differences in cultural background seemed to provide what we both needed at the time: a different way of responding than we were accustomed to.

There were, however, other problems in those relationships that caused their demise. We discovered we were incompatible. But our incompatibility didn't have as much to do with our differences in cultural heritage as it did with who we were as individuals. I'm not sure why those relationships ended. If it was because of our cultural differences, they were only a fraction of the problem. It turned out that in each relationship, both of us realized we were not well suited for each other. There was constant negativity and conflict. Our differences went beyond culture. In one case, we were at different stages of life. She had children, and raising a family with me was not an option for her. For me, raising a family was something I assumed would happen at some point. Neither of us wanted to make a long-term commitment. In another case, we were basically incompatible primarily because our approaches to money were different: she was a spender; I, a saver. I tended to express my feelings and demanded the same from her; she was often overwhelmed by my expression of feelings, and she tended to be more reserved. She didn't want to live with me, and I wanted us to live together, etc.

After these relationships, I met Barbara (who is Jewish). After a few months with Barbara, I knew we were compatible. We had similar goals and values, we wanted the same things, in life and from each other. We were able to talk to each other, and be honest and real with each other, almost all of the time. It was as if trust was a given. The feeling of being perfectly comfortable for us to have differences, heated conflicts -- without threat to the relationship, that we were secure enough to be completely ourselves, with all of our flaws and limitations, was familiar, and at the same time, extremely unique and special. She also had qualities that fit my bill for what I needed from a lifelong partner, one being a nice balance of strength and vulnerability that brought the same out in me. But, perhaps more important than anything else, was what we were able to create together; whether it was understanding, overcoming challenges or accomplishing goals, we did it.

Are the qualities that drew me to Barbara, that make us well-suited, that make our relationship work, attributable to the fact that we are both Jewish?

Probably, to some extent. Our both being Jewish may have something to do with our having similar approaches to money, for example -- not living beyond our means, watching what we spend our money on, trying to get deals on everything we buy. This seems to have made us well matched. Also, she gets along great with my parents and all other family members, which might have something to do with her being Jewish. This has kept issues that are potentially volatile, stress-inducing and relationship-damaging from ever entering the picture. Yet if we didn't trust, respect and accept each other, if we didn't have the ability to be honest and vulnerable, if we didn't value communication and rely on it to resolve our problems, I know we wouldn't be together today. Our compatibility, I believe, has more to do with who Barbara and I are as individuals than it does with our both being Jewish.

When we're dealing with communication and developing intimate relationships, whether we're from the same country, share the same religion, race, interests or philosophies doesn't matter as much as the desire any two human beings have to share their experiences and understand each other.

Don't Limit Your Options!

To successfully practice "**the first date is a clean slate**," the challenge is to keep an open mind. Don't walk into an encounter with ideas about what is or isn't supposed to happen. Give yourself a chance to experience another human being, and allow that person to have an experience of you. See what the two of you can create together!

· · Chapter Five · ·

RAPPORT: A JOINT-EFFORT CREATION

In dating, as with any activity, there is a **primary objective**. When engaging in an activity, everything you do should be aimed at accomplishing this objective. In dating, the primary objectives are **to establish rapport and to get to know each other**. Everything you say and do should be geared toward generating rapport and getting to know each other.

Intimacy Begins with Rapport

Before two people can get to know each other, they must establish rapport. Rapport precedes intimacy.

Rapport occurs when two people are listening and responding to each other spontaneously, not self-monitoring or anticipating what is going to happen. It is a natural unfolding process untainted by the wish for a specific outcome. Both people are "entranced" in a conversation, because the content is personal and important.

The major challenge in generating rapport is observing and participating at the same time, **to maintain an awareness of your reactions and talk about them.** You're trying not to get bogged down in your reactions but rather keep the process going: talking and listening, listening and talking.

If you have ever meditated, you'll recognize the concept of noticing your thoughts while maintaining focus on the simple movement of breathing. When you are focused on generating rapport you are, at the same time, reacting and observing your reactions. You are both involved and uninvolved (or detached). It doesn't matter what thoughts and feelings come up during the conversation because you're doing nothing more than seeing what your and your partner's thoughts and feelings are. At any given moment, you know where you are, but you don't know where you're heading.

Consciously focusing on an objective serves to increase your objectivity and keep your behavior purposeful. It takes your attention away from fears and insecurities, thereby minimizing the extent to which you react based on subjective (more unreliable) phenomena, such as the presence or absence of sexual attraction, projections based on prior experience in relationships and preconceived notions.

The Personalization Phenomenon

The **personalization phenomenon** occurs when you fall into the trap of interpreting the motive for another person's behavior and taking what has been said or done personally. The interpretation you make is usually based on insecurity or wishful thinking. Your internal dialogue may sound something like: "That reaction means he must like me," which becomes a positive self-affirmation, or, "That must mean he doesn't like me," which becomes a negative self-affirmation. When you do this, your response to the other person will be based more on what you think has happened than on what has actually happened. Too often in situations like these, we don't check out whether our perceptions are accurate. In effect, we're carrying on a relationship with ourselves.

If You Need to Know, You Better Find Out!

Mary's way of dealing with her uncertainty about whether a man she liked was interested in dating her was to try to interpret his behavior toward her. This had been going on for a couple of months. Whenever he smiled and spent time talking with her, she got excited and felt more optimistic. But when he'd pass her by, sometimes merely saying "hello" and sometimes not saying anything at all, she believed this meant that he definitely wasn't interested. Hence, these two months had been an exhilarating, but frustrating, roller-coaster ride: "He wants to, he doesn't."

Until Mary got the information she needed, her behavior toward this man would continue to be based on her projections -- on what she imagined his intentions to be.

When she finally mustered the courage to approach him directly, she was still in a quandary:

> "I told him about this new museum and that I thought it would be fun to go see it together. So I asked him whether he'd like to go with me that Saturday. He said that he had plans that weekend but next weekend was a possibility. 'Remind me,' he said. I don't want to remind him! But I didn't say anything about that. Why am I even bothering? I know that he's not really interested in me. This tells me so!"

This situation is common. When you find yourself interested in someone and aren't sure how they feel toward you, there will always be some discomfort. However, if you tend to **"personalize"** the discomfort, you are likely to interpret the other's behavior as rejection and be less inclined to check out whether your perceptions are accurate. Your behavior will be based on mere conjecture, because you don't really know what is happening. This is, for many people, a way of protecting themselves by not giving another person an opportunity to reject them, but instead, doing it themselves. By doing so, they're creating the rejection!

What can you do? The answer boils down to always checking your perceptions for accuracy by asking the other person for the information you need and risking potential rejection.

Mary could go about extracting the necessary information any number of ways. For example, she could say that she wants to make sure she isn't putting him on the spot, and she could ask him whether he really wants to go with her. Or she could be more direct and say something like: "I'd rather not remind you. I'd rather you tell me now whether you want to go this Saturday." At any rate, she needs to hear him **tell** her whether he wants to go. This way, she'll find out sooner, rather than later, what he'd like to do. Maybe he won't want to go out with her, in which case, she'll be dealing with reality. She will know where she stands and proceed accordingly. And only then will there be a chance to generate a rapport and get to know each other.

Handling Criticism -- and Compliments

Many people have difficulty giving and receiving criticism and compliments. This difficulty can result in lost opportunities to ignite rapport or deepen existing rapport.

When it comes to receiving criticism, the tendency is to "personalize" what could be useful information. Your partner is telling you about how he or she is reacting to something you said or did. You might say you want to know how your partner perceives you, what kind of impact you're having, etc., but do you **really** want to know?

If your answer is "not really," chances are you won't be able to respond **freely and spontaneously without self-monitoring or anticipating what is going to happen.** Hearing critical feedback will probably make you react defensively and/or trigger pervasive doubts about your own self-worth -- which will obviously get in the way of rapport.

If your answer is "yes," you will probably find the feedback valuable and appreciate and respect your partner more for telling you. You probably prefer to know where you stand rather than be left in the dark or be misled. You probably have the self-awareness and self-esteem to make use of the feedback. If you don't find the feedback useful, you could choose not respond to it.

For example, when Cary asked June whether there was anything he did that "turned her off," she told him that at times he appeared to be anxious and lack self-assurance.

As a result of June's feedback, Cary became more aware of his own behavior and became more clear about how his anxiety and apparent lack of self-assurance affected June. He made a connection between his self-esteem and how he generally conducts himself during dating encounters.

Cary began the date with June with serious doubts about his desirability. When he took a liking to her, his self-doubts became activated, making him feel anxious and inferior. It turned out that he had exacerbated the situation by drawing attention to his anxiety. He flitted from one subject to another, not with interest in any particular one, but in an effort to cover up his nervousness. His attempt to act like he wasn't anxious when he was caused him to behave unnaturally and unappealingly. And his behavior was largely due to the fact that he couldn't tolerate his feelings of insecurity and was ashamed of them. He wasn't able to think in terms of generating rapport or be creative because he was too caught up in trying to eradicate his anxieties. If only he had allowed himself to feel anxious he would have had the option to talk about it, which might have allowed him to present himself in a different light.

One way to reduce the extent to which insecurity and low self-worth influence your behavior is by learning to reframe your experience so your reactions become acceptable to you. We call this **normalizing.** Normalizing is finding a way of viewing your experience as normal.

In Cary's case, once aware of his nervousness, he could then say to himself, "So what, I'm feeling nervous and insecure. Given my lack of experience, this is how I'm supposed to feel. It doesn't make me less of a person and it doesn't necessarily mean I'll be seen in a negative light." As long as Cary doesn't get consumed by his internal struggles, he'll be able to focus his attention on generating rapport, in which case he will hopefully feel free enough to say something like, "I'm somewhat nervous right now. I haven't been out on a date in a while." This type of communication usually allays our anxieties and restores a natural flow to the conversation.

For most people, giving critical feedback is no easier than receiving it. You are facing the same hurdles as when you're "closing the date" and you're not interested but your partner is -- except there is a bit more at stake when you're being critical, because you're revealing more about yourself.

If you're aware of a negative reaction, such as feeling offended, "turned-off," upset, angry, hurt or afraid, make an attempt to let your date know! Critical feedback facilitates the "getting to know" process.

It might be surprising to learn that more times than not, your feedback will be received as caring. Of course, it depends on how you say it. The point is: if your **intent** is to inform -- not judge or demean -- there's a strong likelihood your feedback will be received in the spirit you intend, regardless of what you say. Furthermore, in most instances, the person on the receiving end of critical feedback has no idea what he or she said or did to offend you. When this is the case, your partner will appreciate and respect you more for bringing attention to it. It's only when we are made aware of how we're coming across that we can modify our behavior. If your partner reacts defensively, this should tell you something about the quality of the rapport, as well as about whether the relationship is worth pursuing.

Although preferable to criticism, handling compliments is also problematic.

A compliment is an expression of appreciation or acknowledgment. Many people can't take praise. Usually it has to do with their level of self-awareness and self-esteem. When they are out of touch with their feelings or have grown accustomed to seeing themselves in a negative light, they fail to recognize and respond to a compliment. They tend to discount or negate anything positive. This creates an unbalanced, "one-way" interaction that usually leaves the giver feeling incomplete, awkward and disappointed.

For example, when June and Mat dated, she shared that she was struck by how wonderful and well-behaved Mat's two children were. She said that what impressed her most was his affection for them and theirs for him and how rare it was for her to see a single father handling all the responsibilities of rearing two children. Mat's reply was: "Yeah, they were particularly well-behaved that night."

Mat didn't respond to the compliment because he has difficulty receiving praise. His lack of response to June's compliment made her feel less involved with him. If, on the other hand, he had said something like: "Thanks. It's something that I've worked hard at and feel proud of," June would have felt heard, Mat would have felt appreciated, and they both would have felt a stronger connection to each other.

When Mat went out with another woman, Ilene, she offered some feedback, which was mostly positive with some negative. He ignored the positive and heard only the negative. Instead of responding to the acknowledgments he received (that she appreciated him for confronting her when she wasn't being completely honest), he focused on what she described as his "mechanical questioning" or "interrogation" about her life.

By focusing on his mistakes and responding with: "I don't know why I asked you all those questions. I guess it's a bad habit," he cut the conversation short. He "dropped the ball," leaving her at a loss. True, she could have sought a response from him that was in keeping with her communication, such as, "Didn't you hear all the things I appreciated?" But why push it? Her impulse might have been to try to make him feel better about himself and compliment him some more. But is this her responsibility? Even if she had ignored his rudeness or changed the subject, there still would have been a void.

When we are talking about quality rapport, these options are "next-best." It is the difference between filling a gap by yourself as opposed to your partner providing the connecting link. Wouldn't you enjoy your partner's participation more?

Here again was an opportunity to bring the conversation to a deeper level of understanding for both people. By expressing her appreciation of Mat, Ilene was conveying several messages that he missed. She was demonstrating a willingness to be vulnerable and was inviting him to be more vulnerable as well. She was telling him what she values in someone she's on a date with -- honesty. Instead of so much questioning, she would have appreciated hearing more about him. And no doubt, she wished that he had responded to her acknowledgment.

When your objective is to generate rapport, it's necessary to make sure the other person knows that you received their compliment. Seeing you register the compliment makes all the difference in the world. Acknowledging your partner and registering your partner's acknowledgment allows the conversation to move to a more personal and caring level.

Due to a lack of communication skills, people commonly encounter problems in giving compliments. Often times, the compliment doesn't come across because of lack of clarity and directness. The person on the receiving end is left wondering, "What is it about me or what did I say or do to give this impression?" and "Who is he talking about?" "Is she complementing **me**?" Perhaps one of the factors contributing to this lack of clarity and directness is the fear of not being responded to.

For example, it was evident Paul wasn't clear enough when he attempted to pay Peggy a compliment. He said, "You're a wonderful woman with a great head on your shoulders." The problem with his communication was that she didn't understand why he said it -- was he giving her a general compliment or referring to something specific?

When Peggy asked Paul to clarify his statement, he told her he was referring to having spoken to her about his troubled relationship with his father. He explained that her ability to understand allowed him to sort out his feelings -- which he needed to do -- and he appreciated her immensely for making it possible for him to do so.

Paul was glad Peggy asked him to clarify his communication because in the process of clarifying, he revealed more of his experience. This not only helped Paul understand himself better, it also helped Peggy understand him. Furthermore, Paul could see the difference it made for her. The clarification made them feel a lot closer.

In both giving and receiving compliments and criticism, the same goals are accomplished. Remember: important and reliable information about each other is what you're after:

Can he take a compliment?

Is she capable of demonstrating appreciation, acknowledgment, etc.?

If there's something I've said or done that he didn't like, will he tell me?

If there's something that bothers me, can we talk about it?

CHAPTER SIX

POLISHING YOUR COMMUNICATION SKILLS

How Do You Generate Rapport?

You must be visible and present.

You must be able to reveal what you're thinking and feeling and how you're reacting, so your partner has a chance to respond to you. It is vital in this process of joint-effort creation that you give your partner the opportunity to respond.

You must also seek revealing information about your partner by asking him or her questions. Then you must listen to your partner's responses.

The quality of rapport largely depends on the ability to listen and respond.

Four basic skills or abilities -- **noticing, self-disclosure, asking questions and listening** -- are skills that must be developed in order to achieve rapport. Just as in any purposeful, goal-oriented activity, certain basic skills are required. In dating, where the goal is to get to know each other, you must be aware, self-disclose, ask questions and listen. The more skilled you are in this, the greater your chances of success.

Awareness Is Your Guide

Self-awareness gives you the ability to accurately represent yourself. If you are **not** aware of how you're reacting at the moment, your responses will not represent your true feelings. **Noticing** what feelings are coming up for you as you interact with your partner determines how well you self-disclose, whether you ask the right questions and how effectively you listen.

Your self-awareness also enables you to respond to nonverbal communication, such as tone of voice, body language, eye contact, attitude, which is essential. What your partner doesn't say is as important as what he or she does say. The more you can tune into what a person **doesn't say**, the deeper the connection you're going to make.

You can use the following questions as a **self-awareness checklist**. You want to be able to answer them at any time during the course of the date.

1) How am I feeling (comfortable, nervous, self-conscious, insecure, anxious)?

2) How comfortable is my partner?

3) What do I want (to say, do or know)?

4) As the conversation progresses, am I feeling more comfortable or less with him or her?

5) Is my partner opening up to me?

6) Am I understood? Do I understand?

7) What positive or negative reactions am I having?

Knowing When You're Disrespected

Perhaps the greatest dating liability is being out of touch with your feelings, especially the ones that tell you that the person you are with or the relationship is not good for you --

that it is downright harmful to your emotional and physical well-being. When you don't know you are being disrespected or that you can't trust your partner, it's because you are cut off from your feelings.

Whenever you're with someone you don't know, there may be always signals, sometimes subtle ones, sometimes not so subtle ones, telling you to "watch out!", "stay away!", "back off!" and "don't get any more involved with this person!" If you're cut off from your feelings, you'll miss these vital signals.

This is what happened when Sarah dated Donnie. She was in trouble but couldn't tell that she was in trouble, that Donnie acted disrespectfully toward her, he couldn't accept her and that she was unsafe with him. All indications were that Donnie behaved abusively and would continue to do so in future encounters. Nevertheless, she pursued further contact, getting herself more involved, thus putting herself in a dangerous situation.

Part of their dialogue went like this:

Donnie: You are a lady who has problems. You don't know whether you are a 'he' or 'she.' I'm not interested in any weird trip like that. (Donnie was referring to a lesbian experience Sarah had disclosed.) I'd rather not spend my time with people like you. I told you that I didn't want to have any friends. Well, that's not true. I just didn't want **you** as a friend... And I'll tell you something else. I was playing in a tournament the other day. I fell in love with a woman who was walking toward me. I didn't feel worthy of her. I said "Hi," and that was it. You see, I knew I was attracted to her because I felt afraid of being rejected. I'm not in love with you and I'm not going to be.

Sarah: How do you know? You never really got to know me. You never gave me a chance.

Donnie's comments, as well as his overall attitude toward Sarah, were laden with contempt and hostility. The tone in Donnie's voice when he said, "You don't know whether you are a 'he' or a 'she'" was entirely rejecting, as if her sexual preference were criminal. He explicitly stated that he did not want her as his friend. There was no inquiry on his part about how Sarah felt or what she thought about her bisexual experiences. He shamed her for not being what he believed was the only correct way to be -- heterosexual.

Particularly striking was Sarah's failure to recognize the potential for emotional and physical abuse in his behavior. There were several verbal and nonverbal messages, or "red flags" that Sarah didn't pick up on. She wasn't able to hear them because she wasn't in touch with feelings of hurt, rage and fear. Had she been aware of how she felt, chances are she would have backed off and refused to be with him. At the very least, she would have recognized that any attempt on her part to achieve understanding with him would be futile.

While Donnie sounded rigid, disinterested and hostile to Sarah's point of view, Sarah never stopped trying to understand what it was about her that was so intolerable to him. She continued trying to convince him that he was making a mistake. She didn't take measures to protect herself, but rather made herself more vulnerable to abuse.

Why didn't she noticed that she was being judged? What caused Sarah to be so dramatically cut off from those feelings that were alerting her to danger?

Sarah had been sexually abused as a child. To survive the emotional and physical trauma of sexual abuse by a family member, she had developed strong psychological defenses at an early age. These defenses served to keep her from being overwhelmed by the pain associated with abuse.

Her principal defenses, repression and denial, had been very effective. Repression had made it possible for her to be completely cut off from the hurt, fear, helplessness, betrayal and humiliation she experienced. It allowed her to survive in the face of the constant threat of further abuse. Denial made it possible for her to radically distort her reality. After she grew up and left home, Sarah remained blank and numb to her horrifying childhood experiences. The blankness and numbness lay at the core of her experience in all subsequent relationships. It became part of the way she related to others, particularly to men. She never learned how to define boundaries for herself or how to maintain those boundaries. As a result, she wasn't able to discern when she was being violated or demeaned in her relationships. This made her defenseless in the face of threats to her emotional well-being. In fact, her tendency was to further jeopardize herself through relentless efforts to get other people to accept her.

For Sarah to have taken measures to protect herself with Donnie, she needed to **notice** his assaultive behavior. To do so would have required that she be in touch with her feelings. She would have been aware of feeling attacked, violated, judged and defensive and probably would have opted to end the conversation without much hesitation. She would have said something like, "I'm not comfortable with your words, attitude and tone of voice. They're offensive to me. You're attacking my choices. It is not okay for you to disrespect and devalue me. I don't feel safe, and I don't want to be around you."

Sarah and Donnie's date underscores the importance of being able to **listen** to another person while simultaneously **noticing** your own feelings and reactions, as well as your partner's nonverbal communication. When you don't have access to your feelings, you are at much greater risk. Your feelings are your allies. They alert you to your vulnerability. Noticing them precedes taking appropriate action to protect yourself.

Contrast how Sarah handled Donnie with Lori, who was in touch with feeling threatened on her date with Harlan.

When Lori confronted Harlan about his being late for their second date, she immediately noticed his arrogant attitude. His justification for being late was "If you would have been more flirtatious and less intense the first time we were together, I probably would have been on time." Lori got Harlan's message -- "I behave responsibly only if I really like or am attracted to you. If not, you're not worth the bother, and it doesn't matter how I behave."

Lori automatically reacted with a feeling of mistrust, anger and avoidance. "Who does this guy think he is?" She felt there was no point in pursuing the conversation, and she told him so.

Your awareness of how you feel makes it possible for you to talk about it, to **self-disclose**. Your awareness of your partner's nonverbal communication can lead to a **question** that invites your partner to reveal him or herself to you. In either case, you will move the conversation to a deeper and more personal level.

During Andrew and Brittany's date, both were bothered by something, but neither talked about what it was.

Brittany was aware of conflicting feelings. On the one hand, she really liked Andrew because he was so easygoing and willing to accommodate her. On the other hand, he was "too nice, like he wasn't there." She felt that no matter what she said, he would continue to be nice. This was frustrating because it made her feel she'd never find out how Andrew really felt.

Andrew noticed Brittany's discomfort but didn't pay much attention to it because he didn't know what it meant, and he didn't feel free to **ask** her about it.

In this situation, the necessary communication is relatively simple and straightforward. If Andrew **asked** Brittany, "Are you feeling uncomfortable?" their interaction would have been different. Brittany would have felt safer and more appreciative of him. Not only would she have felt he was genuinely interested in her, he also would have come across as more sensitive, self-aware and revealing.

For Brittany, a disclosure like, "I'm uncomfortable with all this attention. I'd really like to hear more about you. Tell me about your career," would have worked well. Or, "You seem unusually easy and nice. It makes me think you are holding back. Are you always like that?"

How often have we done this -- notice uneasiness, yet act as if everything is fine?

If you don't risk revealing yourself, you will not discover your partner's response to you. Your partner's response tells you whether you're safe to open up, whether the potential to build trust exists. This is vital information. Certainly if he or she responds with understanding and demonstrates the willingness to reveal more about him or herself, rapport will be enhanced.

Getting to Know You: Self-Disclosure

Self-disclosure means sharing something about what you are feeling at any given moment. It implies consciously taking the risk of revealing your thoughts and feelings because you **want** the person you're with to know about you.

It's a given that you can't control how your partner will respond. All you can do is trust that you will be able to handle it. Although your dating partner's response to you might be disappointing, remember that it's only one date. Your hurt will be short-lived.

In the long-term scheme of things, self-disclosure is actually a viable means of self-protection and cutting your losses. You'll be able to discover sooner, rather than later, that you don't want this person to get to know you or that you don't want to go any further with him or her. This translates into a savings of time and energy.

Many of us regard self-disclosure as being either improper or too risky for a first date. We often try to keep things light and pleasant. This makes sense to the extent that we want to have fun and feel good. We're also trying to protect ourselves from rejection and disappointment. However, when you choose agreeability over being natural, you're keeping rapport from developing and are, thereby, robbing yourself of an opportunity to gain a clearer sense of each other and how you feel about being together. This translates to wasting your time and energy. For example, when Deborah dated Dave, she made a decision to not self-disclose at the beginning of their date. She'd been eager to see Dave but hadn't said this to him out of fear that her feelings would not be reciprocated.

Deborah's decision to not tell Dave how she felt was particularly significant given Dave's pattern of dating behavior. His tendency was to be overly accommodating to make himself more desirable to his dating partner. His modus operandi was to find out what the woman wanted without considering his own preferences. He believed that women wouldn't really want to be with him just for who he was. It would have been an extremely rare experience for Dave had Deborah actually told him she was looking forward to seeing him.

By not disclosing, Deborah kept to herself gifts that when shared would have enhanced her connection with Dave. Sharing her feelings would have not only made Dave feel valued, it would have given him a chance to express mutual feelings.

What and How Much Information Should You Disclose?

In nearly every workshop I conduct, I am asked the same questions: "What does self-disclose or being honest mean?" "What should I reveal about myself?" "How much should I reveal?"

One common-sense guideline is: **Share thoughts or feelings that relate directly to your response to that person at any given moment.** For instance, "I'm glad that I can talk to you and that you understand." Or, "I'm feeling uncomfortable because your tone of voice sounds patronizing." Or, "I don't think you understand what I just said." If you're conversing about interests, values, wishes, desires, dreams, disappointments, fears, goals or politics, that is, if there's a specific topic, talk about where you stand on that topic. Your self-disclosures should be in the context of the conversation.

Self-disclosure doesn't mean sharing all the dark and shameful details of your life with someone you've just met. If, in the name of generating rapport, you arbitrarily select highly personal information to disclose, it's not going to work because it's not part of a natural unfolding process untainted by the wish for a desired outcome. When you're trying too hard, chances are you'll fall on your face. You might feel vulnerable for having revealed too much and then withdraw. Or, if you reveal information that puts you in an unfavorable light, this will likely discourage your partner from wanting to know you and from opening up to you.

Why Can't You Read My Mind?

One of the more common dating pitfalls is **expecting your partner to know how you feel or what you want without you making it explicitly known.** If your partner picks up on how you feel and acts accordingly, he or she rates more highly. If not, "points" are lost.

Despite being unrealistic and counterproductive, many people fall into this pattern, because experiences in family of origin relationships taught them that they are not going to get what they want. In an effort to protect themselves from further frustration, and often times humiliation, these people stopped making their feelings and wants known. They have concluded that if they don't ask, they can't be denied (again). The problem is that when it comes to rapport and gaining a sense of how you feel with your partner, guesswork is not a viable shortcut. **Vulnerability and risk-taking are part of the process.**

Let's say, for example, you and your dating partner decide to go to the beach. Going to the beach has always been one of your favorite things to do. You have the urge to close your eyes and listen to the waves crash against the shore. What would you do?

On her date with Sean, Maureen found herself in this exact situation. Instead of telling Sean what she wanted to do, Maureen said, "I enjoy the beach so much. I love listening to the waves." She hoped Sean would read her mind and join her in silence. But because Sean couldn't read her mind, he never acknowledged her desire. Even though Maureen hadn't given Sean an opportunity to accommodate her wishes, she still felt frustrated and somewhat resentful. She wasn't more direct because she was afraid that if she was, Sean would think she was disinterested, inattentive or perhaps disruptive. She also felt she had no right to ask. As a result, Maureen placed herself into a "no-win" situation.

Asking Usually Means You're Interested

Asking questions is a way to encourage your partner's self-disclosure and move the conversation to a more personal level. You are asking because you want to find out more about how your partner thinks and feels. It is a way of showing that you are interested in someone, which is why many of us like to be asked questions. During a conversation, depending on the questions, asking often makes your partner feel you are really listening to him or her.

Frequently, however, we ask questions not because we're interested in our partner's response but to cover up our own anxiety. We keep the other person busy answering questions so that we won't have to reveal more of ourselves.

Many people are hesitant to ask personal questions because they don't want to be perceived as "prying," "insensitive" or "pushy." Some of this has to do with arbitrarily imposed rules about appropriate topics of conversation for a first date. Given the purpose in dating -- to find an intimate partner, and the objective on a date -- to generate rapport, does it work to "be nice" and "not get too personal"?

It is not unusual for people to be shy about asking questions when they don't completely understand what their partner has said. If they can't read their partner's mind, they often wonder, "What's wrong with me?"

The reason for acting as if we are supposed to know (without being told) goes back to how we were raised. How often were we made to feel uncomfortable for simply trying to understand our parents' behavior or something that happened? After a while, we learned to avoid the overwhelming pain of being ignored, invalidated or criticized by simply not asking and by acting as if we knew. We continue this pattern in our relationships as adults. Taking care of yourself in dating situations means not pretending you know something you don't, and it implies a responsibility to ask questions.

Asking questions often sparks a conversation. Your ability to generate and sustain rapport has a lot to do with the questions you ask. Asking the right questions is one of the keys to feeling more connected to your partner and he or she to you.

Some examples of questions with which to engage your partner are the following:

1) What would you like to do?

2) What is a typical day like for you?

3) Do you expect me to pay for the date?

4) Would you like to get together again?

5) How do you feel about commitment, marriage, children?

6) What would you like to be doing more than anything else?

7) Are you happy in your life?

8) What is the riskiest thing you've ever done?

9) What bothers you about what's going on in the world today?

10) How do you deal with money? What type of money management arrangement would work for you in a relationship?

11) Are you close with your family?

12) Where do you see yourself ten years from now?

13) What kinds of things make you mad, and how do you handle them?

14) What is your ideal vacation?

15) How do you deal with conflicts or fights with friends?

16) What is your ideal relationship?

17) What do you like to do when you are alone?

The idea behind asking questions is simple: **get into a discussion and see where it goes!**

Listening

Listening means your partner has your attention and that you are focusing on his or her experience and trying to understand. To listen effectively, you must be open and in touch with your feelings. Your feelings are your "ears." More than merely paying attention, **the real skill in listening has to do with making your partner feel heard.** It's when your partner feels heard that rapport deepens.

Many of us are unaware that we do not listen well. There are powerful forces preventing us from learning how to listen. One such force is our social conditioning. We have set pictures in our minds regarding what another person is supposed to look and be like. These pictures are often distracting. Rather than listening to what our partner is saying, we are busy assigning points or demerits for appearance and behavior. The tendency is to "judge a book by its cover" rather than take the time to read the pages. Most of the time, we are unaware that we're not really listening.

In the majority of our families, the members don't listen to each other. This is because they don't talk to each other. They don't feel safe enough to reveal themselves. In her book, *It Could Never Happen To Me*, Claudia Black discusses how the injunctions "Don't talk," "Don't feel" and "Don't trust" work as unwritten rules of communication in dysfunctional families. Typically, negative feelings, conflicts and individual differences are either denied, forbidden or amplified to the point where their expression becomes either abusive or cause for engendering abuse.

Furthermore, after a lifelong pattern of defensive behavior, it is easy to completely lose touch with our own experience. When we're cut off from our feelings, our ability to respond in a way that makes our partner feel heard is seriously impaired.

What happens when children from dysfunctional families grow up and interact with other people? When there is any hint of negative feeling, conflict or difference, the tendency is to react defensively. For the most part, this goes on unconsciously. Rather than being able to sit back and listen, a strong need to change or control the conversation kicks in. Instead of listening, we are busy problem-solving or trying to turn negatives into positives. The end result is that the person being listened to does not feel heard.

As a result of these societal and familial influences, negative feelings, conflicts and individual differences are generally avoided in many of our encounters with others. And, if we can't avoid them, we get flustered.

Take a moment to look at your own patterns of listening and see whether you are getting in your own way. When a person reveals that she is troubled by a problem in her life, are you compelled to solve it? If someone is angry about something, do you immediately try to get him to feel differently, to pacify or talk him out of his feelings? How do you normally respond when you're with someone who is scared or sad?

Similarly, when a conflict arises, do you find yourself denying or avoiding it rather than expressing how you really feel? How comfortable are you when differences arise? Are you able to listen openly to your partner's point of view, or are you busy trying to get him or her to agree with you?

Asking yourself these questions should help clarify the extent to which you feel threatened and react defensively in the face of negative feelings, conflicts and differences. It is likely that your defensive behavior can be traced back to early family of origin relationships. You don't want your experience in prior relationships to impede your ability to listen when you are with new people in new situations.

"Don't Solve My Problem. Just Listen to Me."

Andy had gone on many dates that hadn't gone anywhere. No rapport. It became apparent that he didn't have the faintest idea how to listen and respond to a woman who was talking to him about a problem she had. Invariably, he'd try to solve it for her. Alexis, one of the women he dated, gave him the following feedback:

> "After I had some time to think about our conversation, it became clear that you really didn't listen to me. You had an answer for everything. When I shared things that were personal, you tried to make light of it. You were always trying to help me -- giving me suggestions. At the time, I didn't seem to mind all that much because a part of me wants to have someone else run my life. The whole evening was me talking about my struggles and you telling me how to deal with them. But you don't know me. How could you know how to solve my problems? I've been dealing with these issues all my life in my own way. You were more concerned with solving the problem than getting to know me. **I would have preferred that you listened to me, to hear what I was saying, and for you to tell me about yourself.**"

Initially, Andy was confused by her criticism, especially because he had tried so hard to be understanding. He acknowledged that he had been told the same things before by other women but didn't know what to do differently.

Alexis would have had an entirely different experience with Andy had their conversation gone like this:

Alexis: My self-image is that I'm not attractive. I don't believe that men will ever be interested in getting to know me because I'm overweight and always have been.

Andy: It's hard for me to understand because I don't think I ever had an issue with my body. What is that like for you?

Another option would have been for Andy to talk about an issue he was struggling with, such as his relationship with food, sex or anything else that made him feel insecure. By identifying with Alexis through his own struggles, Andy could find a common ground. In so doing, Andy would be demonstrating a willingness to open up and the capacity to relate to his partner.

Alexis would have felt differently had Andy listened without trying to fix her problem, had he responded without trying to convince her that she shouldn't feel the way she does. The problem was that his interest in her didn't come across, which is why rapport broke down. All she wanted was some understanding.

Selective Listening

What happens when you receive critical feedback? Is your ability to listen impaired?

In the following dialogue, Susan asked Bill for some direct feedback, but she had difficulty handling his response.

Susan: I found myself doing all the listening, which is what I usually do when I'm dating. I often wonder whether I come across as boring. **Did you find me boring?**

Bill: Often times when I'm with a woman, I'm afraid of forgetting my thought, so I make sure I say it. I'm also afraid of silence, so I always try to keep the conversation flowing. But you did talk about yourself, and I found you interesting. I loved hearing about you. I didn't find you boring at all.

Susan: But at the beginning you found me boring?

Was Susan listening to what Bill said? She seemed to have misinterpreted Bill's feedback.

Bill said his overall experience was that he enjoyed being with her. He also revealed how, at times, his anxieties affect the way he behaves in dating situations. Her response indicated that she was caught up in her own ideas about herself and wasn't listening to what he said, and as a result, she was unable to hear his feedback or make constructive use of it. It was as if she only wanted to hear the negatives. Maybe Susan believed she was a boring and unappealing person and heard Bill's feedback as confirmation that she was.

Bill then tried to answer Susan's question:

"I wasn't bored when we were together. Since it seems like you are looking for feedback about how you come across, I'll tell you some of my initial reactions. Sometimes you sounded a bit bleak, focusing too much on problems. I noticed feeling depressed after a while. I would have liked it more if you had a more positive outlook."

Susan's reaction:

"I can't stand when someone tells me what I should do..."

Bill was trying to be supportive and to accommodate Susan's request for feedback. The problem here is that as long as Susan is unable to distinguish her own suppositions from Bill's communication, it will be impossible for them to reach an understanding. She will continue to be angry; he will continue to be frustrated.

So Angry You're No Longer Listening

Our ability to listen and respond to other people can be seriously impaired when our partner says or does something that angers us.

When Kaila arrived nearly an hour late for her date with Cary, he was upset. Communication completely broke down because they were so angry, they were no longer able to listen to each other.

>Kaila: It's hopeless. There's no way we are going to work this out. My car broke down. I was extremely frustrated and upset. And when I finally got there, you weren't just upset, you were livid! I tried to explain what happened, that this situation was out of my control. I then asked you, 'Are you still angry with me?' You said, 'Yes.' It took every ounce of energy in me to stay there. I felt hatred toward you. I'm so infuriated with your coldness and inflexibility, I can't listen to you another minute.

>Cary: Yes, anger and resentment had built up during the hour I waited. I wanted to know why you were so late. You alluded to having had a terrible time getting there and being upset about having car trouble, but you didn't care about anything but yourself. The first thing you did when you got there was make a phone call. Then, when you returned, you acted as if I shouldn't be upset at all since you had already told me your car broke down. You didn't take any responsibility for what you did or how it might have affected me. Why should I have cared at all?

Both Kaila and Cary were hurt and angry. Both of them took blaming and defensive positions. Neither person was able to listen to the other and respond to the other's hurt feelings. Their conversation quickly deteriorated, as did their date. If either or both people had articulated some acknowledgment of the other, their date probably would have had a different outcome. If, for instance, instead of focusing so much on the particulars of why she was late, Kaila had been more understanding of Cary's anger, perhaps more apologetic for her lateness, Cary might of been more open to listening to her explanation. Had Cary expressed his anger more explicitly, Kaila probably would have had a better idea of the level of Cary's anger and been able to come across more sensitively. Had Cary demonstrated more understanding of Kaila's frustration over being an hour late and having her car break down, she might not have perceived him as being cold and inflexible. She might not have acted coldly and inflexibly herself.

Cary and Kaila's conflict is a common situation. It can happen with anyone you date and at any time in a relationship. The challenge is twofold: be angry (or hurt) **and** listen at the same time. It's a delicate balancing act to be with your feelings while trying to understand the other person. If you are so consumed with emotion that you can no longer listen to your partner, he or she will have a hard time listening to you. Both people's feelings are equally important, as is their need to be heard.

While breaking communication down to four basic skills may appear overly simplistic to some people, the idea is to know what you need to do to generate rapport. **Self-awareness, self-disclosure, asking questions and listening** -- that's all there is to it. Practice and experience lead to mastery. Being in touch with your feelings is always at the top of the list. Your feelings are your source of information. They tell you when there is rapport and when there isn't. They tell you what to say.

They tell you about the other person. They tell you how to respond. Unless you are in touch with them, you'll be operating in a vacuum.

CHAPTER SEVEN

RELATIONSHIPS BUILT TO LAST

Interest, **honesty** and **understanding** constitute the major components of rapport in any lasting, intimate relationship. The level of interest, honesty and understanding that exists between two people who are together for the first time is the most reliable indicator of their potential for intimacy.

Interest

There are two types of interest. One is **unconditional**. By "unconditional," I'm referring to a level of interest that remains constant. It is being interested in ourselves, in what we are doing with our own lives, as well as being interested in being with the other person. Generally, when we are unconditionally interested, there is a willingness to **play**, to **discover**, **spontaneity** and **adventurousness**. Qualities often associated with "unconditional" interest include **high self-esteem**, **stability**, being **nonjudgmental**, **respectful** and **compassionate**, all of which are necessary in order to achieve intimacy.

The presence or absence of unconditional interest is nothing to be taken personally. It clues you in to your partner. Lack of unconditional interest may be the result of shyness, fear of rejection, depression, low self-esteem, underdeveloped social skills or an inflated value on physical appearances. These emotional manifestations could also signal an addictive relationship to drugs, gambling, food or the like.

The other type of interest is **personal**. Personal interest is interest in each other personally or interest in developing more of a relationship. When you are personally interested, you like him or her, you want to know more about him or her, you enjoy being with him or her, and/or you are sexually attracted.

Of course, we want both types of interest in a relationship.

When there's unconditional interest, it's much more likely that two people will become personally interested. If, however, both people enter into a date lacking interest and are relying on the other person to demonstrate interest first, the interaction can easily bog down into a "waiting game." After a couple of hours of waiting, it's not likely the couple will feel their time was well spent.

I am not saying that physical attraction and the other person's response to you are not going to affect you. No doubt such factors will heighten or diminish the level of your interest. But, ultimately, you want to rely on yourself to maintain a level of interest until the end of the date, regardless of what happens.

In most cases, the lack of either unconditional or personal interest is grounds for not wanting to have a second date (or to pursue a relationship). Which is worse: the lack of unconditional interest or the lack of personal interest in you? In assessing the potential for lasting intimacy, both types of interest must be there.

Honesty

Honesty means being willing to reveal what matters to us, to express what we're consciously feeling, to tell the truth. It is how we demonstrate reliability and dependability. It is how we build trust. If we are not honest with our dates, the conversation will lack substance and there will be no intimacy.

How do we know when someone is honest with us or when we are honest with them? Truth manifests itself as **congruency** -- when overt behavior matches feelings being expressed -- and as **consistency** -- when what is said is followed by the implied actions, by doing what you say you are going to do.

Nowhere is anxiety and fear of being honest more apparent than in dating. Most people are in the habit of avoiding any negative feeling. Often times, if we are in an uncomfortable situation, we'll fumble for the quickest, most palatable and "positive" misrepresentation of our feelings. The tendency is to say what we think the other person wants to hear, not what we're truly feeling. We often prefer to hear things that make us feel good, not what the other person is really feeling.

Take the often-repeated line, "I'd like to see you again." Ask yourself whether you would prefer this to be said regardless of whether the other person genuinely desires to see you again. Does it matter whether he or she follows through with an appropriate action, such as calling you to set a date?

Similarly, would you prefer to hear the truth when it's "I don't want to pursue it," even if you will be disappointed, perhaps hurt? Or do you prefer the position that "no news is good news"? If the truth is not going to be what you want to hear, would you rather avoid it altogether?

Moreover, how do you handle the situation when you are the one who is not sure about wanting a second encounter? Should you say, "I don't think I want to see you again" or would you feel too guilty about possibly hurting the other person's feelings? Would you then say something vague and evasive like: "We could be friends" or "I'll call you some time"?

It might be surprising to know that when we hear "bad news" or have "bad news" to share, it's usually a tremendous relief to get it out into the open. The truth is liberating. By cutting through what are usually emotionally charged, ill-fated hopes, honesty gives us something real to work with, which is empowering in that it enables us to make informed choices. It frees us to choose to go our separate ways, without recrimination, if this really is what we want to do.

Being truthful can also be an invitation for the other person to be open with his or her feelings, which not only makes room for the possibility of our being pleasantly surprised, it can lead to a relationship based on respect and understanding. As we drop our pretenses, we become more visible. We're able to discover aspects of ourselves that would not come out otherwise. We're able to appreciate each other in a way we weren't able to before. Frequently, we value the experience to such a degree that we want to maintain contact with that person in order to experience it again.

In reality, being honest isn't as painful as we often anticipate. When we worry about the consequences of our honesty, it's easy to forget that the truth is liberating. The realization that it has become second nature for us to act differently than we feel (to act **incongruously** and **inconsistently**) should be a lot more painful than temporarily feeling rejected (or guilty for rejecting someone else). Deep down we are yearning for realness, for more depth and contact in our relationships. We want to express our feelings freely and spontaneously. And what a welcome relief it is when we are able to!

Healthy relating in dating means valuing honesty and realness over perfection and appearances. Acting "cool," "suave," "appropriate" or "together" can make you appear shallow and fragile. When the purpose is to develop a lasting and intimate relationship, you are most desirable and attractive when you are honest.

Understanding

The third element of rapport is **understanding**. Understanding is what connects us. It is the interpersonal bridge. I doubt that there's any human need stronger than the desire to be seen, known and understood by another human being.

Understanding requires that we be able to respond, on a feeling level, to another person's experience. It is the ability to empathize with the feelings the other person is expressing. It is seeing "more that meets the eye." It's getting to the life and person behind the words.

The challenge in achieving understanding is overcoming our basic existential condition: that we are all separate and different people. Every one of us experiences the same events differently. It is as if we are all speaking different languages; the meaning of our words is unique to each person.

Meaning has to do not with what was actually said, but with what was meant or intended, the feelings behind the words. **Unless you feel you know what your partner means, and feel your partner knows what you mean, it is questionable as to whether understanding has been achieved.**

Without understanding in our relationships, we remain isolated and alone. The sense of disconnection and emotional barrenness that accompanies the lack of understanding can rob us of life's meaning. Perhaps an even harsher truth is that much of the time we don't realize that understanding has been lacking in our lives until we achieve it. We often need to have the experience to know the extent to which it has been lacking.

The experience of understanding is magical. Regardless of what conflicts or negative feelings are triggered during the course of any intimate relationship, chances are we will feel better if understanding is achieved. While we can't take the feelings away, there is always the consolation that "at least we can understand each other."

For example, on my first date with Barbara, I felt she never gave me a chance. She jumped to conclusions, had expectations and didn't seem to care how I felt. I was frustrated and resentful. By the end of our conversation, she understood that I needed her to **tell** me how she liked to be treated and that she hadn't done this. Rather, she had expected me to read her mind. I wanted her to understand that I really liked being with her -- my "treating" her was my way of expressing this feeling, and she had made it difficult for me to demonstrate my affection in a way that was natural for me. She needed me to understand that being "treated" was symbolic of being special and

A Guide to Creating Intimate Relationships

respected and that she wasn't sure how to measure the existence of these qualities in any other way. In the end, for both of us, it was so gratifying to finally achieve understanding that the conflict and unpleasant feelings disappeared.

The only hope for overcoming blocks to intimacy is your **commitment** to achieving understanding. Unless you are committed, it's unlikely that you'll have the perseverance to get through inherent limitations and differences. Love does not conquer all. It doesn't alter the reality of being human and can't, in itself, bridge the gap that exists when understanding is lacking. You must be committed to the process of achieving understanding in order to get through the pain of isolation. In the context of dating and relating, striving to achieve understanding should become second nature.

After facilitating more than 300 "second encounters" (see appendix), it has become clear to me that those who are committed enough to risk opening up and sharing themselves generally feel encouraged by what they learn about themselves and their partners. Those who don't take the risk or whose need to protect themselves is stronger than their commitment to achieve understanding seem to retain the same sabotaging behavior they started with.

A Misunderstanding

Let's look at what happened between Paul and Emily when a misunderstanding occurred during their date. Although Emily enjoyed being with Paul, he made a statement that tainted her impression. She, however, made no effort to clarify its meaning. When they got a chance to discuss their misunderstanding, their dialogue included the following:

> Emily: The only trouble I had was toward the end when you said 'my two hours are up.' I laughed. I thought it was a great line. And you laughed. But when I said, 'Oh, you don't really mean that, do you?', I didn't get a response. I was under the impression

that you were enjoying conversing with me, but when you said that I wasn't sure. It was an awkward moment for me. I didn't know whether you wanted to stay or go. And I wasn't willing to risk rejection by saying, 'Why don't you come in' and then hear you say, 'Hell no! I put in my two hours.'

Paul: It was just a joke. I think I was somewhat aware that what I said bothered you. What was going through my mind was, 'I hope she doesn't take that seriously.' I really wasn't sure how to respond to you when you said you hoped I was kidding.

Clearly, the way Emily dealt with the mixed messages she received from Paul was ineffective -- understanding hadn't been achieved. No doubt she wanted clarification, but rather than ask Paul what he meant, she waited for him to tell her. Unfortunately, as is often the case, one's dating partner, being unaware of the need for clarification, doesn't give any.

Eventually Paul did recognize his contribution to their misunderstanding and reflected on it later in his dialogue with Emily:

Paul: I do have one little problem. Sometimes I get worried about whether I'm spending too long with someone and am just boring the hell out of them. I do on occasion deal with my anxiety by making jokes. Rather than clarifying, I assume the other person understands. If you had asked me if I wanted to spend more time with you, I would have said, 'Sure.' I was just going to watch a football game with this guy, but it wouldn't have been a problem to change my plan. I would have said, 'Heck yes, I want to come in.' But I see that I caused confusion by not letting you know that, yes, I enjoyed myself and wished to spend more time with you, but had other plans.

Paul and Emily's situation is an all-too-common occurrence. They had different expectations regarding their date. Paul assumed that he would spend two hours only (from ten to twelve o'clock) and made plans to watch a football game at one o'clock regardless of how much he enjoyed himself. Emily didn't set a time limit. The irony was that they both liked each other, yet each felt the other wasn't really interested. After they talked it out, they saw that they both had been wrong.

Intimacy Works in Mysterious Ways

Your ability to achieve understanding depends largely on your commitment. But even when your commitment level is very strong, there's no guarantee that you won't have to deal with some painful and reactive feelings. Simply understanding your partner doesn't provide you with the ability to foresee all of the issues and conflicts you will face with people you are dating.

One example of not being able to predict how you or another person will react when intimacy has been achieved came to light in a conversation I had with Bruce.

Bruce found himself completely baffled, and somewhat hurt, when seemingly intimate encounters with two women took unexpected turns. He described the following scenario in which he and the first woman shared a "phenomenal rapport":

> "We talked about sex and relationships. I felt a strong bond there. We were really close. Then I called her for weeks afterward and left messages, which she never returned. I haven't heard from her for over three months. She's just blown me off. I couldn't understand it. So finally I called her one more time to find out what had happened. She told me that she'd gotten scared and had backed off."

The other experience Bruce talked about was with someone he'd been seeing for a couple of months:

"She'd call me when she was emotionally upset. My natural response was to be with her and support her. So one night I went and stayed at her house. We talked together on a really deep level. I felt very close to her. She actually **told** me how grateful she was to have me there. We held each other all night long.

"Then, a couple of days later, I got a phone call from her saying she needed to take a break from me. She didn't want me to call her for a while. So I told her 'okay,' if that's what she wanted. But it's been almost three weeks, and we haven't had any contact. She told me that because she probably hadn't gotten over her last boyfriend yet, any other intimacy felt too scary for her right now.

"I just don't understand that. I'm not that way at all. I crave intimacy. I want to know why other people are so afraid of it."

First, let's focus on how Bruce's "craving" for intimacy might have caused him to lose sight of the degree of real intimacy he'd actually achieved with each of these women. Very likely it was Bruce's innocence and naivete that caused him not only to misinterpret the depth of contact they'd experienced, but also to not notice how each woman had reacted to the level of intimacy that actually had been achieved. After spending a whole night holding a crying woman, it's reasonable to interpret this as an intimate experience, but if she had frequently cried in men's arms, doing so with Bruce might not have been special to her. If, on the other hand, she opened herself up too much, too soon, she might have felt a need to step back.

Our perceptions are a function of what we feel inside and of unconscious emotional needs. What Bruce described happens all the time. When we are desperately seeking love or wishing to "fall in love," as so many of us are, we tend to inflate or deflate the significance of any one interaction. We lose the "one date at a time" approach to developing relationships and project into the future. In order to keep ourselves in check, it helps tremendously to approach every date (whether it's the first, second or thirty-second) as if they are "clean slates."

In Bruce's case, he assumed that sharing intimacy with a woman at any given point in time necessarily means that she desires further contact. He took for granted that more appreciation would be expressed by her the next time they were together and that they would become just as intimate again. Bruce believed that because he'd had a "bonding" experience with a woman, he would be permanently bonded with her.

Although seemingly logical, this is not how intimacy works. It occurs at the time two people are together, not beforehand. It does not necessarily carry through from experience to experience. It has to be jointly created each and every time two people are together.

The fact that two people are interested and honest with each other and want to achieve intimacy doesn't mean that those elements will be present each time they are together. The idea is to be in the moment and cherish every intimate encounter you share with someone rather than hold an assumption that this quality of rapport will automatically repeat itself in the future.

There are so many factors that affect a personal encounter. The set of circumstances at one point in time that promotes interest, honesty and understanding may not be there the next time we encounter someone. For instance, when on vacation many of us tend to act far more freely and spontaneously because we're not following the life-style we're accustomed to. So if we meet someone while traveling, we'll probably relate to that person differently than we would if we were out with them on a typical Saturday night date.

An intimate encounter can literally shake us up, especially when our experience is scant. In most families, as well as in our society, intimate relationships are extremely rare. An intimate experience can act like a drug experience in which we get "swept away" and lose sight of how vulnerable we've been.

Later, we may realize that we've opened ourselves up more than we intended. We may need to create some distance from the person we opened up to in order to feel safe again.

Most of us are not even intimate with ourselves. So when we realize we've shared things with another person that even we weren't aware of, such as things we are ashamed of, we may feel acutely exposed and out of control. This situation is intensified if we've come from a dysfunctional family in which defensive behavior is second nature. This is why an unexpected experience of intimacy often produces a delayed fear reaction and a need to restore a sense of inner safety. Making ourselves emotionally and physically unavailable for a while may be the only option we have to accomplish this.

Because the experience of intimacy is one of vulnerability and one we generally are not used to, there's no way to know how a person will react to an intimate experience. Be prepared for some repercussions! Notice your feelings as they come up. Then stop and check in with the other person. If you become aware of a strong sense of closeness, say something like, "I'm really enjoying feeling close to you. How do you feel?" The only way two people can fully share an intimate experience is if they are conscious of their feelings and express them.

For Bruce to learn from these experiences and protect himself in the future, it would help for him to voice something along the lines of, "I've been intimate with women before who later avoided me." In addition to being realistic, such communication can call attention to insecurities in the other person that they may not have been aware of, let alone been able to express.

Intimacy vs. Sexual Attraction

Many people question whether **interest, honesty and understanding** are in fact the elements that make relationships work. Sexual attraction and the physical chemistry that exists between two people, coupled with alignment of interests and philosophies, are considered to be the primary forces that bring people together. These considerations, however, are frequently exaggerated to the detriment of a developing relationship.

"You are worth pursuing only if I desire you sexually" reflects an attitude that not only sabotages rapport but also the potential for an intimate relationship.

When Elliot was ending his date with Isadora, he said to her:

> "I really liked being with you. You have beautiful eyes and a great smile. I wanted to be with you to get to know more about you…But when it was time to go home, everything began to change. I thought about seeing you again. Then I did what I always do: ask myself, 'Am I sexually attracted?' My answer was 'No.' I wondered what to do. If I wanted to follow up, I would have had to ask you for your phone number and that would have implied that I wanted to pursue it."

For many people, a great time is often not good enough. When our primary motivation and criterion is sexual attraction, we can wind up devaluing rapport, which is what Elliot did. Because great rapport without sexual excitement was not much of a motivator for Elliot, the possibility of developing a bonafide friendship was lost.

Yet in the process of exploring his feelings, Elliot saw that he had been afraid:

> "I just didn't know how to deal with this type of situation. We could have become friends and a sexual attraction might have developed. But I didn't think so. I thought I'd wind up hurting her. It's like I have to know the future, otherwise it's too dangerous to explore it."

Elliot's inability to tolerate ambiguity and his fear of the unknown affected his behavior. His way of achieving a sense of security to delude himself. How could he know what would or would not happen before it actually happens? What if they continued to have a quality rapport, and he did become sexually attracted to Isadora? The mere possibility of hurting her feelings because in the future he might never become sexually interested in her was enough to deter him from developing a friendship.

"Why are you so afraid of developing a friendship with someone you're not initially sexually attracted to?" I asked Elliot.

"It's been pretty heavy. I've had many of those types of relationships. After a while, I'd get to the point where the woman would feel that either there was something wrong with her or something wrong with me. I felt pressured. We wouldn't talk about it. It would get increasingly more uncomfortable. And then we'd stop seeing each other."

Naturally, we tend to avoid situations where there is a potential for getting hurt, but being so afraid that we avoid becoming intimate is unnatural and antithetical to our purpose in dating.

In Elliot's case, his behavior had more to do with his lack of experience in discussing the lack of sexual attraction than the lack of sexual attraction itself. He hadn't yet learned how to communicate his feelings, how to find out about the other person's feelings and achieve an understanding. The only way Elliot can learn to cope with his fears in a healthier, more effective manner is to be honest about them. Once understanding becomes an option, the "pressure" will decrease, and so will the intense discomfort and shame.

The lesson here is that if your desire to see each other again is based entirely on sexual attraction and you don't focus on the quality of rapport, it is less likely that you will develop an intimate relationship. The fact is that there is little correlation between sexual attraction and intimacy. It is actually more likely that sexual attraction will develop when rapport is established than the other way around.

In any intimate relationship -- like a cozy home -- interest, honesty and understanding can be found dwelling in every corner. Whenever these qualities are present during a first date, sustaining them within the context of a long-term relationship will always be easier. For all its apparent complexity, the real mystery and magic of any intimate relationship derives from only three ingredients: interest, honesty and understanding. They are the glue that holds a relationship together.

CHAPTER EIGHT

RATE YOUR DATE: THE TEN CRITICAL QUESTIONS

These are specific questions that will help you accurately assess the potential for intimacy with someone you're dating. Remember, **the ability to achieve mutual understanding** is the key to establishing a long-term, intimate relationship.

There are ten questions you should always ask yourself in order to assess "intimacy potential":

Unconditional Interest

1) Was I focused, motivated, ready to relate in the present?

2) Was my partner ready to relate?

Personal Interest

3) Was I interested in her/him? If so, how?

4) Did he or she act interested in me? How did he or she show it?

Honesty, Realness and Depth

5) Was I honest? How did my partner respond? If I wasn't honest, why wasn't I?

6) Was my partner honest and willing to be personal with me?

Understanding

7) Did I feel understood by her/him? How?

8) Did I understand her/him? What specific things did I learn about my partner?

Another Date?

9) What is my overall feeling toward this person? Do I want to see her/him again?

10) When and how am I going to convey that I want another date?

These questions are designed to help you evaluate the quality of rapport you've achieved with the other person. They are questions that can only be answered on a feeling level. Answering them requires self-awareness, being in touch with your feelings, being accustomed to introspection and capable of assessing levels of mutual interest, honesty and understanding.

It is possible that even after addressing these questions in the manner suggested, you will still be unable to access your true feelings and responses. Under these circumstances, you may want to consider seeing a therapist to work through whatever personal issues are standing in your way. You don't want to be in the precarious position of depending on another person's reactions to you in order to evaluate how you feel about them.

Unconditional Interest

QUESTION # 1: Was I focused, motivated, ready to relate in the present?

It's essential that you take a reading of your own level of unconditional interest -- did you want to be there? If you went on a date feeling depressed, tired or preoccupied after a hard day at work, you probably weren't in a position to be optimally responsive. If you were feeling depressed or insecure from other stresses when meeting someone for the first time, it's possible that not even the most wonderful person in the world would pique your interest. It's also likely that you'll find it difficult to assess the level of the other person's **unconditional** and **personal** interest.

QUESTION #2: Was my partner focused, motivated, ready to relate in the present?

The level of passion, enthusiasm, optimism and unconditional interest your date displays is a sign of health and well-being. Showing interest in life, having some passion, goals and purposes are usually reflections of high self-esteem. These are people who feel that what they are doing with their lives matter.

Paying attention to the way people feel about what they say will enable you to learn much more about them. Does your partner appear anxious, depressed, overly pessimistic or cynical? Notice how you feel as the other person talks about him or herself. Do you feel more interested and stimulated, or less so?

Often times we have difficulty assessing another person's level of interest in themselves. Once again, it's a matter of being in touch with our feelings and reactions.

For example, even though Brad had been talkative, Helen perceived him as not really being interested in what he was saying. His talkativeness was much more obvious than the actual content of what he said, and it certainly didn't indicate he was interested in her. Not too surprisingly, Brad hadn't noticed Helen's interest either, because he was so busy talking.

However, when given an opportunity to look more closely at their individual experiences, each began to see things differently. Helen recalled how Brad seemed to come to life during their discussion about movies. Brad remembered how passionately Helen had spoken about horseback riding. While reflecting in this way, each touched upon a feeling of genuine interest in the other.

Personal Interest

QUESTION #3: Was I interested in her/him? If so, how?

While assessing whether you felt interested in a person you've gone out with, strive to be as objective as possible. For example, when you're sexually attracted to someone, your interest usually has more to do with sexual excitement than with how you actually felt being with him or her. Be sure to check yourself: "Was I sexually attracted? If so, did my interest go beyond sexual attraction? What specifically caught my attention about him or her?"

QUESTION #4: Did he or she act interested in me? How did he or she show it?

When you're on a date, you want the other person to be as interested in you as you are in them, without having to do anything to qualify for it. The main point is to be conscious of your desire for another person to show interest in you. In virtually all of the **Dating To Relate** workshops I've conducted, there has been a primary, recurrent issue: one or both of the dating partners feared that the other wasn't truly interested (or if there was interest, that it hadn't been clearly demonstrated).

When you think about your wish for another person to be interested in you, it's important to make a distinction between being liked and true interest. True interest is more akin to respect for you as a human being. If, as the date unfolds, the other person becomes personally interested in you, it's even better. And, of course, if you are interested in him or her, it's better still.

Many people are not aware of their need for another person to be interested and respectful. What often happens is that when we are assessing our dating experience, we'll sense something awry but not know what it is, which is why it's necessary to always ask ourselves, "What did he do (or not do) that made me feel he was interested (or not)."

For example, when Helen was exploring her experience, she realized what she missed during her date with Brad: "I guess what I wanted was some kind of attention from you -- yeah, that's my word for it -- attention, on me."

When you are sexually attracted to someone you've gone out with, it's harder to reliably assess the other person's level of interest in you. The tendency is to lose sight of how you actually feel with and about that person. Therefore, it is important to separate sexual attraction from intimacy. Ask yourself, "Was this person sexually attracted to me? Did his or her interest go beyond sexual attraction? What specifically, did he/she say or do that made me feel he was interested?"

What you're looking for here are the qualities of reciprocity, mutuality and balance. You want to know that your interest is shared more or less equally. You want to feel that this interest flows easily. What you don't want is the interest to be focused mainly on one of you.

When there is an imbalance in giving and receiving attention during an initial encounter, it can indicate that the developing relationship is driven by unconscious emotional needs. The two people will tend to behave according to an unspoken but mutually agreed upon emotional contract; "I'll take care of you as long as you continue to like me. And I'll like you as long as you take care of me." In contrast, an intimate relationship develops from a sense of trust and the experience of understanding one another's needs and feelings.

If your date appears more interested in you than in himself, this could be a reflection of low self-esteem. Perhaps he doesn't feel satisfied in his life or maybe he's keeping the focus on you out of fear. It is also possible to habitually focus more on the other person than ourselves in order to be liked, and, as a result, we do not learn to self-disclose. It's very difficult to generate rapport with someone who isn't revealing, who doesn't share or who is depending on you to "talk about yourself" first.

If, on the other hand, your date focuses most of the attention on him or herself, that could indicate self-centeredness and imply a limited ability to see, understand and respond to you. This person may be more concerned with getting attention or impressing you than with finding out who you are.

Honesty, Realness and Depth

QUESTION #5: Was I honest? How did my partner respond? If I wasn't honest, why wasn't I?

QUESTION #6: Was my partner honest and willing to be personal with me?

When you address the issue of honesty, remember that your honesty is your responsibility. If you see that you weren't honest, ask yourself why -- was it because you didn't feel safe with him or her? Is it that you don't find it easy to open up to people in general?

If your difficulty in being honest with your dating partner comes from caution about opening up, it will be hard to get the information you need to assess the quality of your dating experience. If you haven't been able to be open, how can you accurately evaluate how you felt? It's necessary that you give your date an opportunity to respond to the "real" you!

It is safe to assume that if your date doesn't reveal his or her thoughts and feelings or share personally with you, there is little potential for intimacy. Intimacy depends upon mutual willingness to share experiences. Again, I'm not suggesting that one reveal painful, very personal details of one's life on a first date. Rather, you want to assess the other person's level of honesty in the natural flow of conversation.

Being honest increases the chance that two people will establish rapport. By choosing to make your feelings known, you'll be able to handle negative reactions so that they won't escalate. Unexpressed resentment usually turns into unexpressed criticism, which usually leads to more unexpressed resentment. Before long, you'll hate this person!

In addition, by being honest, you'll gain a sense, right then and there, of his or her ability to respond to you. You'll see whether this person takes responsibility for his or her behavior, and you'll get a glimpse of how well you can problem-solve together.

Mutual Understanding

Question #7: Did I feel understood by her/him? How?

Question #8: Did I understand her/him? What specific things did I learn about my partner?

Understanding is the heart of the matter. It is our most basic need in a relationship. If you feel the conversation flowed, that there was mutual interest and honesty, and that you were able to understand each other, there is good reason for further contact.

You always want to ask yourself, "Did I feel heard by my date?" "Was what I shared about myself accepted without judgment?" Consider whether you felt any rejecting, contemptuous or condemning feelings in how he or she responded to you. And were you accepting of those things that were not what you were expecting or hoping for in your partner?

If, during a date, either of you makes an attempt to reveal something in an effort to be better understood, but nothing "clicks," chances are this is a sign of things to come. Similarly, if we find ourselves unable to relate to or accept our partner's point of view no matter how hard we try, this is a problem.

Another Date?

Question #9: What is my overall feeling toward this person? Do I want to see her/him again?

Question #10: When and how am I going to convey that I want another date?

I've had the following dialogue with group participants more often than I can remember:

Member: We didn't go out again.

D.L.: Why?

Member: He probably didn't want to be with me. Maybe he didn't have a good time. Maybe I did something wrong.

D.L.: Did you ever let him know that you wanted to see him again?

Member: No. I never thought of it. That's a wonderful idea.

Is this really a "wonderful idea" or just common sense? So often we don't follow through. When we don't know the truth about something, we make an assumption. We fail to recognize that in order to have a second date, we need to take the necessary action to find out whether our feelings were mutual so we can proceed. We have to discuss it!

Bringing resolution to your date is the key to feeling good about it, regardless of the outcome. Too often, we leave things unresolved; we don't discuss our desire to get together again. Instead, our tendency is to wait until our date makes the next move.

A decision to ignore the situation, even if unconsciously made, usually comes as a result of not acknowledging our true feelings. So the question of whether you want to see your date again just hangs there. Either you will whimsically choose to see each other again, or you will whimsically choose not to.

One way or the other, you won't have a solid basis for your decision.

After you've considered whether you want to get together again, you should ask yourself what you intend to do about it. How will you let your date know what you have in mind? Are you prepared to make a phone call to let the person know you want to see him or her again? The important thing is how you left it at the end of the date. If you said you were going to call but that isn't what you really wanted to do, will you just forget about further contact? If you left it open, then not having any more contact may be consistent with the communication between you and your date.

Exception to the Rule

There's always the possibility of unconscious forces sabotaging a person's pursuit of an intimate relationship. Hopefully, the principles of healthy dating and relating contained herein, as well as the questionnaire, can serve as guidelines for building healthy relationships. However, they can't ensure that readers will be able to go out and turn all of their dates into intimate partners.

There is always the potential for self-deception and wishful thinking. No matter how honest and serious you are in answering these questions, you are influenced by your unconscious emotional needs. This can often result in the misinterpretation of another person's behavior.

Bonnie presented a perfect example of how the answers to these questions can be misleading. She expressed doubt about the reliability of her answers to the questionnaire regarding a dating experience. "If I had honestly answered these questions to myself, every answer would have led me to pursue him."

To the first question, "Did my date act interested in me?" she responded, "He acted interested in me. He took hold of my chin, looked into my eyes and told me what a special person I was. He also said that I had a good soul and that he could fall in love with me."

Does a demonstration of interest on a date normally include such effusive compliments and romantic innuendo? Not necessarily. No doubt Bonnie found it hard to differentiate between actual interest and a flirtatious come-on. For her, flirtatious behavior signified not only that a man really liked her, but also that they could share a future together! She was totally unaware of her tendency to hear only what she wanted to hear, while censoring any contradictory messages. This impaired her objectivity. His compliments and romantic posturing were apparently exactly what she wanted from him.

As Bonnie considered the question, "Did he show interest...," she replied: "Sure. He invited me to join him at his next music gig. He wanted to sing to me."

Yet Bonnie wasn't certain whether this invitation represented a genuine interest in sharing part of his life with her or whether he was more interested in trying to create a good impression.

Odds are this man was merely attracted to her and wanted to get her in bed as soon as he could. The way Bonnie described their conversation definitely sounded as if he was trying to seduce her. Bonnie also said at one point that she'd wanted to be wooed and to have sex with him.

Bonnie's response to the question, "Was he more interested in me or in himself?" focused only on the attention she'd received from him. She had little to say about how he presented himself. Yet each time he told her how wonderful she was, she "melted" and became even more attracted to him!

Bonnie was also operating with a hidden agenda -- she admitted playing "hard to get." She said, "Although I felt really interested in him, I was afraid to show it because he might have gotten scared."

There is a belief system at work here. It suggests that if we risk showing our interest in someone, we'll automatically scare them away; therefore, we'd better not act interested unless the other person shows interest first. Bonnie played "hard to get" in order to not be rejected. Being pursued was clearly the surest and safest way to protect herself, because it allowed her to completely avoid taking any risks.

It's likely, though, that on a deeper level another issue was at the base of Bonnie's behavior. She might have felt unworthy of a man's attention (or perhaps anyone's attention). Therefore, it would have been too painful and risky for her to expose her feelings only to find out later that she'd been right.

Bonnie revealed more about her internal process of assessment when she dealt with the questions about mutual honesty. She admitted, "I didn't think he was honest because his stories seemed farfetched and unrealistic. But I didn't give it much thought. I wanted to believe him very badly." As long as her partner expressed what she wanted to hear, she didn't care whether it was true, because that would have threatened the attention she'd been getting. She never considered the level of her honesty with him, which made it appear that she had no intention of being honest.

Bonnie's response to whether she had felt "understood" was simple: "Sure, he understood me. He constantly told me how terrific I was. I felt like he understood my deepest needs."

With regard to whether she learned anything about him as a person, again she framed her answer in terms of her wishes and desires, "He was coming from 'wanting' me...being super-attracted to me...wanting to spend more time with me to get to know me better. I learned that he was assertive, self-assured, persuasive and persistent. That was very attractive to me." She made no mention of his work, life goals, experiences in his family or any other relationships.

As one might expect, Bonnie's answer to whether she wanted to see her date again was, "Of course." Her action plan? "I'll let him know that I'm available," she said, "so he'll come after me."

When asked what came of this relationship, Bonnie said with a note of surrender in her voice, "I saw him for a couple of months. Sex was fantastic. I really thought he cared about me. But all of a sudden he left town. He never called me again. I still don't even know where he is! And what's more, he gave me herpes... What can I say? My body and my need to be pursued spoke louder than my need to know who this guy really was. I just wanted it to be how I wanted it to be. I didn't care what was real. Otherwise, there would have been nothing to look forward to."

How reliable were Bonnie's responses to the questionnaire? Bonnie's pattern had been to evaluate her interactions with men based on the degree to which they expressed interest in her, particularly interest of a sexual or romantic nature. As long as men made her feel wanted, she liked them, which was why she was unable to differentiate between strong rapport and sexual excitement. Additionally, she had a tendency to seek confirmation of her desirability through sexually focused conversation. Her behavior during the date, as well as her assessment of it, was more a function of her unconscious need to create emotional distance than a desire for real intimacy. This unconscious need was so powerful that it distorted her sense of reality, making it impossible for her to accurately interpret what was happening.

The process Bonnie went through teaches us that we can never take our perceptions for granted. There's more than meets the eye. Bonnie's deep yearning to feel special, adored and wanted mirror similar feelings in all of us. At one time or another, we all trick ourselves into believing that we're receiving a nurturing kind of attention when we're not. While we may wish there was a way to overcome our self-destructive tendencies and free ourselves in order to create an intimate relationship, we are, at any given point in time, limited by our level of emotional development.

Part Two

DEMYSTIFYING SEXUAL ATTRACTION

CHAPTER NINE

OVERVIEW OF THE MOST COMMON PITFALLS

No Attraction, No Interest

Unless we feel sexually attracted to the person we're dating, our interest tends to wane. Usually a lack of energy accompanies this disinterest. What the other person is saying simply doesn't matter as much as when we are sexually attracted to him or her. What we are saying matters little to us as well. Our interest in being with the person, our interest in finding out about him or her, and whether we have a positive or negative experience, is overly dependent on the presence or absence of sexual attraction.

The inflated significance of sexual attraction is also evident when it comes to assessing the character and compatibility of the person we're dating. It doesn't matter that we have spent no more than an hour with this person! For example, you might feel so excited that you act giddy and silly, laughing at everything your partner says to you, and then surmise that he or she has a great sense of humor. You might feel profoundly enlightened when he or she talks about his or her job simply because you've never met anyone who worked in that field before. You could easily trip off into a "happily ever after" future together merely because both of you value a physical activity such as bike riding. All kinds of wondrous possibilities explode in our minds. Very simply, there seems to be a shortage of other criteria when assessing our dating experiences and selecting relationship partners.

Reality Can Be a Drag

Most of us aren't aware that when we are sexually attracted to someone, our imagination is running wild. The problem isn't that we're fantasizing, it's that most of the time we don't know that we're fantasizing!

Often times we don't want to know that what we are imagining is not reality. Even when the tendency to inflate the significance of sexual attraction is brought to our attention, many people still rely on it as the primary criterion. Even when we recognize that our perceptions tend to get distorted, and are, therefore, unreliable to use in assessing an encounter, our tendency is still to hang on to sexual attraction as if it was the only criterion. Why do so many people repeatedly fall into the same trap when they know it is a trap?

One reason is the level of dissatisfaction in our lives. When we are in pain, any opportunity to relieve or escape the pain is one we don't often refuse. When we are emotionally malnourished in our relationships, when we lack meaning and a sense of purpose, sexual excitement or intrigue is much more appealing than focusing on developing an intimate relationship.

Another reason is the lack of experience in intimate relationships, which makes it more difficult to distinguish between excitement and genuine rapport, between what is intimacy and what is not.

Feeling and Acting Are Not the Same

Many people are afraid of feeling attracted to another person and are also afraid to tell him or her that they are. They do not allow themselves to experience the excitement that accompanies attraction and cringe at the idea of another person knowing that they have sexual feelings.

As a result of our cultural and familial conditioning, we often lose sight of the fact that the feeling of attraction and our decision to act are completely separate issues. When we can't separate our feelings from the decision to act on them, feelings of powerlessness, of being trapped, vulnerable, obligated or guilty are liable to get triggered. To avoid these feelings, many people simply do not allow themselves to experience or express sexual feelings.

Jennifer presented a dating situation she wanted some direction about. She had difficulty making the distinction between her feelings of attraction and deciding whether to act on them.

"There's a man with whom I've developed a friendship and am attracted to. I don't know what to do. He invited me to a party that is so far away that we were going to stay at his place overnight. Yes, I'm attracted to his mind and body. But he's got other relationships going, and I'm not ready to get physically intimate with him. I don't want to get hurt, and I don't want to ruin it because I really like him."

Jennifer's experience makes us think about how to handle the situation when we are attracted to someone but are not ready to act on those feelings.

Whenever you're attracted to someone, it is a matter of handling two things at once. You want to be aware of your attraction and enjoy the accompanying excitement, but you also want to be able to assess whether acting on those feelings will be in your best interests. This can be done as long as you make a distinction between your feelings and your decision-making process. Even when you are attracted, it is possible to carefully **assess** the situation in terms of whether you want to **act** on your feelings. The decision is yours!

Do not lose sight of how well you know this person and the amount of time you have actually spent together. Ask yourself, "Do I feel ready to get sexually involved?" "Do I feel as emotionally connected as I do physically?" "What are my fears?" "What are my expectations?" "Are they realistic?" In most cases, initiating a discussion about your concerns will facilitate your decision-making process. You need to know whether you can talk about your feelings, and whether this person is capable of understanding, respecting and accepting how you feel. This information should tell you what course of action to take.

Establish the basis for an intimate relationship first, and worry about sex later!

For example, Jennifer could say, "I'm attracted to you (and perhaps desire to sleep with you), but I don't think it would be a good idea for me tonight. Staying in separate beds tonight feels right."

Jennifer then voiced another concern: "I'm afraid he'll take my saying I'm attracted to him as an invitation."

More likely, he'll take it as invitation if she goes ahead and sleeps with him. If she emphasizes her needs and history in relationships and he still expects her to sleep with him, it may be time for her to pack her bags and go home. During the course of conversation, Jennifer might see this man as someone who doesn't understand or care what she feels or thinks.

By expressing sexual desire while not acting on it, saying for example, "I'm attracted to you but want to sleep in another room," Jennifer would be accomplishing several things at once. She would, in effect, be affirming herself -- "I am a healthy woman. I have sexual feelings, and they're wonderful and exciting. And I have other needs, too." By mustering the courage to stand up for herself and tell a man how she feels, she'd be exercising her freedom of choice, which is empowering. It would also give her a much clearer sense, after the man responded to her, about how safe it is for her to be truthful. Perhaps most importantly, she would be allowing herself to experience physical and emotional excitement while simultaneously protecting herself and creating a space for intimacy to occur. No longer would sexual feelings pose a threat to her emotional well being.

Low Self-Worth

Another important distinction is between your self-worth, your feelings of attraction and how another person responds to them. When your self-worth depends on whether your feelings are reciprocated, letting another person know that you're attracted often becomes a risk not worth taking. When reciprocity is taken as a measure of your value as a person, you've lost perspective. Self-esteem is a separate issue. It should be internally based and fairly constant, not determined by how another person responds to you.

Shame

Feelings of shame are another difficulty in allowing ourselves to have sexual feelings and to reveal them. When we're ashamed of our sexuality or our bodies, we often suppress sexual feelings. And suppression is only the tip of the iceberg. When it is drummed into our heads that sexual feelings are bad and wrong, we suffer humiliation for having them. When we have been constantly criticized, punished, rejected and misinformed, we learn to reject or deny our sexuality in order to protect ourselves. The whole gamut of feelings, including joy, sadness, fear and anger, is left denied, rejected or unexpressed.

"Splitting" Sexual and Emotional Intimacy

For many people, sexual intimacy and emotional intimacy don't go together. They put themselves into an either/or situation. If they have sex, they will not be emotionally intimate. If they are intimate, they will not have sex or allow themselves to have sexual feelings. Some people have never been in a relationship that was sexual and intimate.

Kelsy is a woman in her forties who never had both a sexual and an intimate relationship. Her yearning for a romantic lover, an intimate partner and perhaps a husband had grown stronger with each passing year. She had made a concerted effort to deal with her frustration and find out what kept her from developing a relationship in which there was both physical and emotional chemistry.

Let's look at how Kelsey's attitudes and behavior fostered the split between sex and intimacy. Regarding her date with Devon, she said:

> "I had a great time with him, felt safe and really appreciated his openness, but I'm not feeling 'romantic' toward him. I'm purposely not thinking 'romantically' because my concepts of what I'm looking for have changed. I am in the process of redefining what 'romantic' is and what a potential relationship is for me.
>
> "If I was sexually attracted to someone, I thought this could lead to romance. I was 'off the wall,' thinking so idyllically. I had watched movies and saw people walk off into the sunset and thought that was what I wanted. I didn't know that it wasn't real. But it was what I wanted! Now, men are real people to me, not ideals.
>
> "I don't want to think romantically anymore because I'm afraid if I do, then I'll slip back into my old patterns. I spent the better part of my dates hoping I was attractive enough. But even when a man was attracted to me, I still didn't feel a connection. I can see why that was happening. I was so caught up in my own fantasy world, there wasn't anything to connect to. I wasn't there."

Kelsey realized that when she had been dating she was in a fantasy world and that now that she was ready to make a change, she had gone to the opposite end of the spectrum, completely denying her sexual feelings. By segregating her emotions from her body, she was putting herself into a bind whereby she'd feel either emotionally intimate but not sexual, or sexual but not emotionally intimate.

To avoid falling into the trap of splitting sex and intimacy, you must be aware of several things at once. You want to focus on the quality of rapport and the level of understanding that has been achieved and, at the same time, allow yourself to have sexual feelings.

If you deny sexual feelings, you won't be able to express that part of yourself when it's natural for you to do so. If you say to yourself that you are not going to have sexual feelings (or any feeling, for that matter), you will not embrace yourself wholly. This translates to a negative affirmation -- "I can't face sex, my body, my feelings -- so I'm not going to."

It would be healthier, more complete, whole and real if the sexual feeling was there naturally **and** you were able to say so without going off into La-La land. You can try thinking along the lines of "I'm attracted to you. It's not that big a deal. My sense about a potential relationship doesn't revolve around it." You want to validate your sexuality and feel proud of it.

Besides, you can't take the feelings away. All you can do is deny them. And, if you deny your feelings, you are at greater risk of losing yourself in a fantasy, because the fantasy can become an easy means of avoiding feelings. It's only in the idyllic, romantic scenarios of your mind, where everything happens as you wish it to, that you don't have to deal with your fears and insecurities. Again, it will help you if you make a distinction between your feelings and the decision to act on them.

Dirk described his "split" between sex and emotional intimacy when he said the following:

> "I find it paralyzing to say to a woman that I'm not attracted to her sexually or romantically. Part of it is that I know how much it hurts me when I hear that. Out in the real world I'm feeling like 'Oh, please love me.' For me, relating has been a game of trying to win approval.

"It's very difficult for me to set limits with a woman. Being honest and setting limits have always cost me. Saying I'm not sexually available to them is one of the ultimate limits. My whole life has been geared for serving women -- my mother and then two wives. If I had been able to tell a woman I wasn't really attracted to her, I would not have gotten married a second time. I did (and still do) love her as a human being, but don't think I was ever sexually attracted to her. I was taking care of her. I was her 'messiah'."

Dirk's "split" had to do with his not feeling like he had a right to his feelings. Beginning with his relationship with his mother, he learned to act as if women owned him. He gave his decision-making power to women. Invariably he'd do what he thought was expected or what the woman wanted without considering his own feelings because he felt they posed a threat to the relationship. As a result, he tended to deny his sexual feelings and never had a truly intimate relationship.

For Dirk to overcome his deeply ingrained pattern of giving up his power and sexuality, he must, at some point, find the courage to say that he's not sexually attracted, if this is the case. He must be honest and set limits early on, during the first date if necessary. By taking these risks, he will eventually come to validate himself.

When we are honest about how we feel, we are, in essence, saying, "This is who I am. I am not here to take care of you while ignoring myself." Behavior consistent with our purpose reinforces the purpose. We want to foster relationships in which we feel secure enough to set limits and express our wants and needs without the threat of losing the relationship.

Sex, Flirting and Romance

To enjoy the excitement of sexual attraction safely -- that is, without impairment to your decision-making ability -- it will help to understanding three related phenomena: **sex**, **flirting** and **romance**. These are particularly troublesome because they are so often mistaken for intimacy.

Nothing More Than Sex

The ability to feel sexual attraction, to become sexually aroused and to have sexual relations is part of our biological makeup. If we are in healthy physical condition, these abilities occur naturally. We know that sexual arousal is an extremely pleasurable sensation. When we view sexual experience from a strictly biological standpoint, there's nothing mystical or magical about it. We can have sex. We do have sex, and there aren't many things more enjoyable. It is only when sex is confused with intimacy that it becomes problematic.

Confusion is evident in the words we use to describe sexual encounters. Most of the time, when we say, "we were intimate," or "we made love," the truth is that it was nothing more than sex. We live in a culture in which "being intimate" or "making love" and "having sex" have become interchangeable. The distinction between them has gotten lost.

One explanation for this confusion is that when we're physically naked it appears as if we're intimate and vulnerable, while on an emotional level, we're really not. Emotional sharing and understanding are harder to achieve, which makes sex the thing we prefer to do first simply because it is easier and feels better.

It is also likely that seeing ourselves as strictly physical, sexual beings is too demoralizing. Most people would prefer to see themselves as not being ruled purely by instinctual or libidinous impulses, because in our culture, mature adults aren't supposed to act that way. As a result, at those times when we are primarily interested in having sex, not necessarily an intimate relationship, we can't admit to ourselves that it is sex we're after. So we have sex, but we call it intimacy. We delude ourselves into thinking the relationship is an intimate one, expect our partner to act accordingly and be hurt when we find out that "it was only sex he or she was after."

A common misconception is that emotional intimacy will naturally accompany or follow sex. Even great sex in no way guarantees emotional intimacy. The two are separate entities. For many people, sex becomes great when emotional and spiritual connections accompany it. For them, great sex is actually more likely **after** emotional intimacy has been achieved.

Often times, making sex the primary goal is a way of protecting ourselves from being vulnerable. In those instances when emotional intimacy threatens our sense of well-being and control, focusing on sex works to dissipate our anxieties. Once again, the underlying need to self-protect runs counter to the goal of achieving intimacy. When this is the case, sex, not the ability to be intimate, often becomes the basis for the relationship.

"Look at Me! I'm Sexy!"

When we are attracted to someone, it is common for us to flirt. However, if you don't know **what** flirting is or **when** you are flirting, you're more likely to misinterpret the communication or be misinterpreted. When flirting is mistaken for intimacy, you run the risk of making decisions based on false assumptions.

Flirting is an indirect, nonverbal way of piquing another person's interest and desire, to engage him or her by sexualizing the communication. We can flirt consciously or unconsciously.

Flirting allows us to feel open while investing very little emotionally. It is a game two people play at being close, without really being close or revealing themselves. We might say things like, "She was really nice," "He was really neat," "We had a great conversation" or "We had a really strong connection."

Like sex, flirting is both physically and emotionally exciting because it appears as if there's a high level of interest. Again, there's nothing inherently bad or wrong with flirting. It's actually quite effective because it does what it is supposed to do --

generate excitement and interest -- especially when there's mutuality. Only when it's mistaken for wonderful rapport or intimacy does it become problematic.

Flirting can lead to a relationship in which flirting characterizes the style in which two people relate to each other. It may lead to an evening of great sex. It can also lead to the kind of relationship that revolves around sex. It can, but rarely does, lead to an intimate relationship. The only way it is possible for flirting to lead to true intimacy is if the people involved are doing so **consciously** and when flirting is only one facet of an otherwise honest and open exchange.

Many of us are proud of our success in the art of sexual flirtation and seduction. Yet rarely do we realize that when we play games of this nature, we are off purpose. A far more challenging modification to the "look how sexy we could be" game, one that is in keeping with developing an intimate relationship, would be to add, by tacit mutual consent if necessary, "Okay, so you're sexy. But what else can you show me about yourself? What else can I show you about myself?"

Just You and Me, Forever

Romance is another facet of sexual attraction that is problematic for many people.

The state of romance or "being in love" is a peak experience. It can be summed up as follows: "Everything about you, I like. Your eyes, your hair, the way you speak, the way you look at me. There's nothing I don't like. I feel better with you than anyone else. I love you more than I ever loved anyone. We're perfect together. I want to be with you all the time. Not being with you is unbearable. Everything we do together is wonderful. Sunsets. Gazing into each other's eyes. Touching. Loving." Sound familiar?

The question is, how long does it last? What many people fail to realize is that like any other peak experience, the state of being "in love" is intense but temporary.

If being in love is what you are ultimately after, chances are the relationship is doomed. You will not be prepared for the reality of each other's shortcomings, differences and feelings. You will not be able to cope with the inevitable fall from grace.

To enjoy the experience of being in love and, at the same time, stay in reality, it helps to ask yourself, "Do I want my partner to be my ideal or do I want him or her to be who they are?" "Do I want to be my partner's ideal, or do I want to be myself?" It's far less likely you will "crash" if you are able to make a distinction between what you want and what is possible. You don't want your partner to be flawed or limited. You don't want to be flawed or limited yourself. But if you can not accept your own or your partner's limitations, the prognosis for a lasting, intimate relationship becomes quite bleak.

Also ask yourself, "Do I ultimately want to 'fall in love' or do I ultimately want someone I can love and who loves me?"

If your answer is "yes" to the former, the relationship will probably have some great highs and lows, but in the end you may have nothing to show for it. So often I hear that because "I'm not in love" or "He or she is not 'in love' with me," something must be terribly wrong with the relationship. Wanting to be "in love" all the time is dangerous, because its very nature is temporary.

If your answer is, "I ultimately want both," then the only way it will be possible is if you make a distinction between the two **and** if you are committed to being real and honest with your partner.

Sometimes Learning the Hard Way is the Only Way to Learn

Recently, my friend Brenda shared with me a letter she had written to her close friend, Molly. She wrote it the day after her first date with Joe. The date turned into a night of flirtation, romance and sex. Brenda's letter serves as a great example of how the excitement of sexual attraction, when coupled with flirtation, romance and great sex, can lead to unhealthy choices and disillusionment.

Dear Molly,

Well, I'm in love. Remember my friend Bob gave my phone number to this guy? Well, he phoned last week and we met Monday evening. His biography -- 32 years old, in sales in the garment district in New York, happily married parents, married sister, ex-jock, went to Penn State on a football scholarship; fairly good-looking, receding hairline, great body; super personality, amazing combination of macho, strong, bulky, and soft, sensitive and loving.

Well, he called me Monday morning. The temperature and humidity were brutal, and I knew that he needed to be nurtured, which made it a perfect opportunity to invite him for dinner. He called me to say that he was running late, only fifteen minutes. Most guys are expected to be at least fifteen minutes late anyway. He came over with a terrific bottle of wine. Conversation played easily for both of us, like we had known each other forever. After a while, I suggested the roof. He hadn't made any moves on me, which I liked.

We got on the roof and it was gorgeous and romantic. We sat where I am now -- a higher spot on the roof which affords an amazing view. I brought up a blanket and we sat and talked from 11 p.m. until after 3 a.m. We talked very intimately about out lives, lovers, loves, etc. He had a girlfriend all through high school and college, and they broke up. She married and divorced and so on. We kissed a few times, and it was yummy. And lots of cuddles.

Upon returning to my apartment, he sat on the table and made no advances. I finally said, "Let's get comfortable on the bed." We laid down and kissed. Great kisses. The sex was simply unbelievable. He told me I was the best lover he ever had. We fell asleep at 4:30 a.m. and had to wake up for work at 7:15 a.m....

Brenda thought she was in love. She never saw or heard from this man again. Like millions of single people, Brenda wanted more than anything in the world to find someone and get married. However, her relationships with men for the past several years had been much like the encounter she described in her letter.

Brenda was stuck in a pattern that would inevitably leave her feeling dumbfounded, lonely and hopeless. There were long periods when she took a break from men. But when loneliness and boredom set in, she continued in pursuit of "the one." When her experiences turned out to be as exciting as this one, she felt lucky.

One might think that Brenda would have learned after a while. But learned what? That she shouldn't get sexually involved so fast? That great sex is nothing more than what it is and certainly is not an adequate foundation upon which to build a relationship? That she needed to learn how to relate intimately? That she was living in a dream world?

Evidently, the forces operating in Brenda were stronger than her common sense and nullified the impact of a string of disappointing experiences. She used sexual attraction, flirting, romance and sex for occasional excitement and relief from the pain of loneliness. Sex had become a means through which she felt loved. She had a need that could not be denied. Because the need to be loved for who she was (not how well she performed sexually) was still very much alive in her, it was practically predetermined that she'd confuse any orgasmic experience into one of being in love. She may not have known how to relate to a man in any other way.

Brenda felt sexual attraction, flirted, felt romantic and had great sex in one night, but that was all she'd gotten. If she had seen Joe again and continued seeing him, it would have been a relationship based on her fantasy of Joe as she felt he should be. It probably would have been the same for him. There's no indication that she would not have continued to mistake lovemaking for intimacy. During their date, had she been aware of her unbridled excitement and had she instead paid attention to the quality of rapport (particularly the elements of honesty and understanding), she might have written a different letter to Molly, perhaps something like the following:

Dear Molly,

I met this guy through a friend. I invited him to my house. We sat and talked for hours. He's really attractive to me, great body, fairly good-looking, intelligent and sensitive. He seemed to open up to me, but it was only one time together. I feel that there's a connection. Maybe he's going to be the one!

I was flirting. He was flirting. I could have made love with him. I know that it would have been unbelievable. Given my history, though, that wouldn't have been too smart. I've learned a lot about myself: that it's easier to act seductively than to stay in touch with my feelings. I really liked him. It was quite the challenge not to flirt. I was definitely uncomfortable. I think he was, too. He really wanted me.

What if he does really like me, then what will I do? I'll see how I feel after being with him a few times, so I have more to go on than one nice evening. We'll see if it feels that good again and again; at least several more times. Then I'll have a better idea of what's happening. There's just no way of knowing at this point. I think it would be great, but if I proceeded on that basis, I know I'd be in big trouble.

Oh, I want him so badly I can't tell you. But it was so great just to be able to talk to a man and feel understood and have him open up to me! It was great just being together and feeling so engaged. I wonder what it will be like the next time we're together...

CHAPTER TEN

CUTTING THROUGH THE MYSTIQUE

There may not be a more mystifying phenomenon than sexual attraction. When we are sexually attracted, our perceptions, motivation, thoughts, feelings and behavior are all profoundly affected. There's no question that we are tantalized by the desire to be sexually attracted to someone else and to be sexually attractive to that someone.

The purpose of this chapter is to cut through the mystique and explain what is actually happening when we are sexually attracted to someone.

Our Bodies, Our Sexuality

From a physical standpoint, there is nothing mystical or magical about sexual attraction. Feeling sexually attracted, the accompanying bodily changes, as well as the ability to have sex are part of our biological makeup.

When this biological need is not allowed expression, the result is a buildup of frustration or pain. The greater the degree of frustration, the stronger the need for immediate sexual expression. It follows, then, that the stronger our need to relieve sexual frustration, the greater influence this need will have on our behavior. Whether we are aware of it or not, everyone goes through life with a certain amount of pent-up sexual frustration.

Because human beings live in relationship to other human beings, it is in the context of a relationship that our sexual need will or will not get met. The need to satisfy our sexual drives often distorts our perception of the quality of the relationship. The level of intimacy that actually exists is always open to interpretation. Unless we are aware that we are having a relationship in order to relieve pent-up sexual frustration, or simply because we want to have sex, chances are we will make more of the relationship than it is. And, unless we have had experiences in intimate relationships -- for a basis of comparison -- our tendency is to delude ourselves about the level of intimacy that actually exists. In either case, we are more likely to make choices based on what makes us feel good at that moment than on the level of intimacy achieved.

Our Emotional Needs

We also are born with a wide spectrum of emotional needs that must be expressed in our relationships. Our need for emotional nourishment is as powerful, if not more powerful, than our need for a sexual outlet.

As children we have a wide range of emotional needs that must be met in our relationships with adults for us to grow and become emotionally healthy adults. We need to be responded to in ways that make us feel safe, wanted, special, that we matter, and that give us a sense of belonging. We need to feel that the people around us, those we depend on, understand, accept and respect us.

Generally, in healthy families, in which members feel close and bonded to one another and the expression of love flows naturally, these needs get met.

In unhealthy, dysfunctional families, a good many of these needs do not get met. However, when we are children, we are unaware of these needs and don't have any way to know if they are getting met or being denied. If they are adequately met, our development progresses, and it is more likely that we will be able to express ourselves freely and spontaneously. If they are denied, our emotional development will stagnate. Our energy will instead be used up defending against the pain, cutting off our feelings. As a result, in adulthood we will remain unconscious, both of our needs and of the pain caused by needs not being met.

The same dynamics that apply to physical needs apply to emotional needs. Our emotional needs are always alive in us, seeking expression and gratification. When they are denied, there's a buildup of frustration. The more frustration and pain, the stronger the need becomes, and the more influence it has over our motivation and perceptions. We will be drawn to others who respond to our unconscious emotional needs and attribute our attraction to other factors, such as character and compatibility, thereby distorting the quality of the relationship. Because the distortion process itself goes on unconsciously, we have only our experience in intimate relationships to bring us back to reality.

Our Imagination

Our imagination is as basic to the human condition as are our bodies and emotions. It helps us cope with frustration and reduce stress. The frustration stemming from unmet physical and emotional needs is the driving force behind our imagination. The level of pent-up frustration determines how much a role our imagination will play in our day-to-day lives. The more frustrated we are, the more we rely on our imagination.

At the point at which this pain becomes intolerable, an elaborate array of psychological weaponry can be called upon. Included in our arsenal of defenses is our imagination, which is capable of supplying images that act as substitutes for the real thing. This gives us the power to tailor our perceptions to suit our needs, which distorts our sense of reality.

The level of excitement associated with various images often has to do with specific unmet needs and the level of frustration associated with them. The more frustration there is, the more excited we get. It doesn't matter that the images amount to nothing more than a fantasy; they are real to us. It doesn't matter that they do not provide real nourishment, we still feel better.

The imagination works on both conscious and unconscious levels. When it is unconscious, which is the case most of the time, what we're imagining is experienced as reality. It is not until a disillusioning event occurs, one that forces us to confront reality, that we realize that our imagination was operating.

For example, unless and until Brenda (who wrote the letter in the previous chapter) realized she wasn't going to see Joe again, it would have been virtually impossible for her to see that she was deluding herself about who he was and what their relationship was. When we are aware that our imagination is operating, the distinction between what is real and what is not is clearer. We know that we are fantasizing and therefore, are less inclined to act on a fantasy.

Sexual attraction occurs on both a **conscious and unconscious** level, and it involves the blending of what is **physical and emotional**, **real and imagined**. Our bodies are aroused (conscious), our imagination is operating and unmet emotional needs are being tapped (unconscious). The overall effect is synergistic. The physical aspect is compelling enough as it is -- we know we are attracted because our bodies are telling us so. What we don't know is that our imagination is adding an emotional dimension to the experience that further intensifies the excitement.

In his book, *Self and Others*, R.D. Laing talks about the synergy that occurs when bodily excitement combines with the imagination. He says, "real bodily excitement together with imaginary experience holds for many a fascination mixed with horror." He explains how a relationship with an **imaginary** other develops and how it can undermine the development of relationships with real people.

Laing uses the behavior of masturbation* to illustrate his point. The masturbator relies on his imagination to achieve an orgasm. Although the masturbator's imagination induces real (physical) effects, they are different from the experience of having sex with a real person. Once accustomed to the orgasm of masturbation in imaginary situations with imaginary people, he will become increasingly unsure of himself in real situations. For instance, he may expect a woman to be the way he imagines her while masturbating and may be confused if she acts differently.

The same principle applies to sexual attraction -- real bodily excitement mixes with imaginary experience. Not only are we physically excited, our imagination is operating (unconsciously). Most of the time, we prefer to stay unaware that our perceptions are inflated, because seeing the person in a more realistic light would "rain on the parade" -- excitement would be lost. Nevertheless, the excitement comes at the expense of objectivity. Rather than relating to (and getting involved with) the actual person we are with, we are relating to emotionally charged images of the person as we wish him or her to be. Not only are we unable to distinguish between reality and fantasy, we proceed with a sense of certainty.

In a nonexcited state of mind, the process of assessing the person and/or relationship changes dramatically. Our perceptions and way of thinking will be based more in reality and we will feel more vulnerable. Recognizing that no one is "perfect," that there are and will be things about the person we won't like, that negative feelings will come up, that there will be con-

---

To clarify intent of discussion about masturbation -- nothing negative regarding the practice or behavior of masturbation is implied. The reference to masturbation here is to serve as a concrete example of when and how fantasy and reality can become merged.

flicts and rough times, brings our doubts and insecurities to the surface. We will wonder whether this person is right for us, whether we will be compatible, whether the relationship will last, with no way of knowing what the future will bring. Hopefully, our assessment and ultimate decision to pursue the relationship will not be based on how attracted you feel, but rather on other factors, such as the level of honesty and openness, ability to communicate, feelings of trust and respect.

It is probably safe to surmise that what Laing was referring to when he used the word "horror" was how vulnerable we are when fantasy is confused with reality. It can become impossible to have an intimate relationship. It can become impossible to make reality-based decisions. We can have experiences we wish never happened, find ourselves in relationships we'd be better off without.

The potential for "horror" occurs when there is a backlog of pain stemming from unmet physical and emotional needs, when the imagination becomes a substitute for what is missing. Rather than relying on the imagination to provide a safe, occasional diversion from the stresses in our lives, it becomes our primary means of relief and our primary relationship. Overreliance on the imagination is a vicious cycle. The more involved we are with imaginary others, the more frustrated and isolated from real people we become. The more frustrated we become, the more we take refuge in our fantasies and the more exciting they become. And we can't break free because we are unconscious. Even if we are forced to confront reality, we are left with the grim task of dealing with our pain without the means to relieve it. In no time, we will be seeking other avenues of relief.

Remember that the ultimate goal whenever you are dating and are sexually attracted to the person you're with is **to enjoy the excitement without letting it impair your ability to create intimacy.** Your top priorities are developing a healthy, lasting relationship and maintaining a perspective on reality. To accomplish this goal, you must be able to make the following distinctions:

- between sexual attraction/excitement and intimacy,
- between fantasy and reality,
- between the excitement and the decision to act.

Distinguishing Fantasy from Reality

One way to better understand the distinction between fantasy and reality is to consider the following questions: **Would you like to have an affair?** and **Would you have an affair?**

Two different questions, both so volatile in nature that most of us prefer not to think about them. In addition to clarifying the distinction between fantasy and reality, my purpose in asking (as well as answering them for myself) is to shed light on what might be the greatest challenge in developing and sustaining an intimate relationship: **acting responsibly in the face of desire.**

I've been happily married for eight years and have two children. I am strongly committed to my vows of fidelity. I'm a therapist who specializes in building intimate relationships. Yet I recently found myself poised precariously on the edge of the forbidden zone -- the opportunity to have an affair presented itself.

It was one of those days I would have liked to stay in bed with the covers over my head. I woke up feeling depressed and disconnected. As the day wore on, I felt increasingly stressed out, frustrated, downtrodden and totally alone. I'd describe the state of mind I was in (but not aware I was in) as apathetic and reckless -- perhaps desperate for some excitement or relief. I was at my office and had a half-hour break before my next client. What was I going to do?

I thought, "Why not make a trip to the mailbox and get some fresh air?" On the way, I stopped at the candy store around the corner to say "hi" to my friend Susan who worked there.

On occasions when I had gone in to get candy, we spent several minutes chatting and eventually developed a sort of friendship. Our initial conversations centered on the many flavors of chocolate in the store, all of which were given out as free samples on a regular basis. Then the topic shifted to movies. Then to my family members (whom she had met at various times during the year). Then to her boyfriend ("an okay weekend relationship"). Our encounters were always spontaneous. They eventually became quite playful, and our playfulness got physical to the extent that we'd hug each other.

There probably was an underlying but unexpressed attraction between us. I can't even say whether we had acknowledged these feelings to ourselves. They became clearly evident to both of us, however, one particular time. We hugged, and her face turned a bright red. We both laughed and went on with business as usual. This brief, seemingly innocuous interaction turned me on. I was surprised by how physically aroused I got. Not only did this experience make me more aware of our mutual attraction, but my imagination got activated as well.

On this day, it wasn't candy I wanted. I was looking for more excitement than that, but all I was conscious of seeking was one of those warm, full-body hugs, something to lift my spirits. Susan was there. We hugged, and as usual, I got aroused. I got what I came for, so I proceeded on my walk to the mailbox. During my stroll, I started fantasizing about having sex with her.

Just as I was about to enter my building I spotted her walking across the street from the opposite direction. I was amazed because it seemed impossible that sufficient time had passed for her to be where she was. As she was walking toward me, I thought how great it would be if she came up to my office. What if I asked her to come up? Would she want to come up? Would she get it on with me? Do I have enough time? I stood there waiting for her to approach, frozen in fantasy. I wasn't sure what to say to her. Feigning surprise, I yelled, "How did you get so close to my office so fast?" Apparently, she didn't hear what I had asked her. She responded, "You want me to see your office?" It was as if she had heard me thinking. "Yeah," I said. "That's a great idea!"

There we were in my office at ten after five (and a client scheduled at 5:30) -- enough time for us to have sex, albeit a "quickie." We seemed to be at a loss for words and fumbled through the obvious small-talk about how nice my office was, etc. After a few minutes, she looked at me and suggested it was time for her to return to the candy store. I didn't know whether I was disappointed or relieved. After a few seconds of hesitation, I agreed. "I guess you have to get back," I said. As she left I stood there wondering, "What if she closed the door of my office and said, 'O.K. You want me? Now you can have me!'" I don't know what I would have done.

Even the first question: **Would you like to have an affair?** -- the more benign one -- makes my heart palpitate. A voice in the back of my mind tells me that my answer is not supposed to be "yes," that people who are happily married, committed to vows of fidelity and who are entrusted to guide others on matters of the heart should not think about having affairs. But there is another voice telling me that it is perfectly all right to **want** to have an affair. "My wishes and desires are my private business. It's not like I **did** anything. Besides, how uncommon is it to **fantasize** about having an affair? The idea must cross everyone's mind one time or another."

So the truth is, "Sure, I'd like to have an affair." Given the right conditions, I can't think of anything more exciting. It depends on how I'm feeling. When I'm deeply frustrated and stressed out, the fantasy draws the most attention and is most tantalizing. But when I'm feeling satisfied in my work and relationships, it's a different story. I'm not looking for an escape. I'm too busy doing other, more important things to be bothered. It goes from one extreme to another. Some days, there's nothing I'd rather think about, and some days the thought never enters my mind. Clearly, it depends on how replenished and fulfilled I feel.

Imagine for a moment, what it would be like to have an affair. For me, it's the ultimate fantasy -- a sexual interlude in which I am not encumbered by inhibition. One in which there's no emotional baggage whatsoever for either one of us: no conflicts, differences or negative feelings. She expects nothing from me, and I expect nothing from her. There's nothing about her I dislike, and she wants me unconditionally. She knows exactly what to say and do without my telling her. She just knows. She is the safest woman on the planet. I can open up about anything, and she'll comfort me with understanding. There's no one like her. It's the same thing every time: we can't wait to make love, the love-making is more wild and passionate than any I've ever experienced. Then we part with no guilt or obligation, only with appreciation and anticipation of our next encounter, whenever it will be. There's no such thing as stress when we're together -- it doesn't exist. No stress!

Could having an affair with Susan be this good? Perhaps. If it were this good the first time, would it continue to be so in subsequent encounters? Doubtful. Simply because reality can not match our fantasies. Reality and fantasy are two different realms. Yet, they are connected.

An analogy: you're in a desert in the sweltering heat without water, and all you can think about is an oasis. Then you see one, and you're ecstatic. Unless you were in a desert dying of thirst, you wouldn't experience excitement or desire. Under normal circumstances, "oasis" would be just another word, a purely intellectual concept having no emotional impact.

We fantasize about things that are missing in our lives -- which is why fantasy works so well as an escape. If things weren't missing, we wouldn't be fantasizing about them. We wouldn't be as excited or feel as much desire or be as compelled to act.

If, in my mind, Susan had been anything other than a fantasy figure, I wouldn't have been at all excited by the idea of having an affair with her. The moment the fantasy resembled reality, involving a real person with real needs, a real relationship with the ups and downs that go with it, there would have been no incentive to have an affair. The only reason I had the fantasy was that I wanted nothing to do with reality.

My "close call" with Susan had less to do with Susan the person than it did with my need to escape my pain, which, relatively speaking, was quite substantial at the time. Clearly, my imagination and the accompanying excitement was nothing more than a temporary reprieve from how I was feeling at the time, which was sexually frustrated, emotionally isolated and stressed out.

Fortunately, I didn't push it. I knew my fantasy wasn't going to translate in reality, that the actual experience would fall way short of how I imagined it. Somehow, I knew about the buildup of excitement, the orgasm and then the crash. I knew that at the core of my excitement was a need to escape, and I had relied on my imagination to provide it. Apparently, the fantasy was enough for the time being.

I also knew that fantasizing posed no risk unless, of course, I couldn't distinguish my fantasies from reality, and I acted based on this confusion. What helped make it possible for me to make the distinction was my willingness to acknowledge my wishes and desires regardless of whether I considered them impossible, forbidden and outright wrong. Acknowledging them enabled me to see them for what they were -- just fantasies, wishes and desires. It also helped to have some understanding about how our imagination works. I knew that if my wishes and desires remained unconscious, I'd be at much greater risk of projecting them onto other people.

Even though my understanding of what my excitement was all about influenced my behavior, in that I never initiated sexual contact with Susan, that doesn't mean that if the opportunity were to present itself on another occasion, and I was in the similar state of mind, that I would necessarily act in the same way. So if the situation did present itself, **would I have an affair?** Actually having an affair is a far cry from wanting to or fantasizing about having one.

Anything imaginable can be acted upon. However, the moment a fantasy is acted upon, it is no longer a fantasy, because real people are involved.

In the first case, I was poised precariously on the edge of infidelity. Had I acted on my desire -- if Susan and I had actually had sex -- I'd have fallen over the edge. I'd be dealing with a whole different set of consequences.

For one, the nature of our relationship would have changed from platonic to sexual, from friendly acquaintances to secret lovers, with no way to undo it. Furthermore, whether it had been a onetime occurrence, a sporadic or a regular one, I would have either had to lie to maintain the affair or confess to my wife. Concealment would create a wedge between my wife and me that would probably increase as time went on -- especially if the onetime occurrence became a more frequent occurrence. Undoubtedly, confession would precipitate a monumental upset in our marriage. Either of these scenarios posed undesirable consequences.

I wish that my understanding about how imagination works and my ability to assess the potential consequences of my actions were enough to make me say "no" to this question, but they aren't. The voice in the back of my mind is saying, "Don't incriminate yourself!" The truth is, however, I **could** have an affair. If I was sufficiently run down and the opportunity presented itself, I'd be walking a tightrope. It doesn't matter how happily married I am or how high my integrity or my status is. I know that when I'm feeling depressed, apathetic and frustrated, I want immediate relief. I don't think about consequences. In a weak moment, I can act impulsively. Furthermore, if Susan and I had had sex that day, I'd probably have kept it a secret. I could deny this dark part of myself, the part that can lie to get what I want, but I'd only be deceiving myself.

Knowing the part of myself that was capable of dishonesty and self-deception, and in this case, betrayal, made me take nothing for granted. Being aware that I was totally capable of putting myself into a situation that I'd regret later made me carefully assess the situation and decide not to act on my impulse. Even though I was left wondering "how great it would have been" and became more aware of my inconsolable pain at the time, I was glad I didn't have to deal with Susan after sex. I was glad to not have any guilt. I didn't lie, and there was no crisis to deal with in my marriage.

The fact is that every one of us can have a breakdown. If and when it happens depends on how conscious we are. When we go through life seemingly intact, yet are not in touch with our dissatisfaction and pain, we are walking time bombs. The odds are it will be only a matter of time before the right person comes along and the opportunity to place ourselves into an unhealthy situation presents itself. The rest will be history -- our desire will be all-consuming. We will idealize the other person and the relationship and blind ourselves to the impact it will have in our lives.

Consciousness is desire's worst enemy. It warns us about deluding ourselves when we don't want to be warned. It reminds us about consequences when we want to believe there won't be any. It tells us we better wait when we are desperate for immediate relief. It appeals to our decision-making agency at the most inopportune times. Then, suddenly, we find ourselves responsible for how we act when we don't want to be!

What do you get for deciding not to act on your desire?

There is power and strength in acting responsibly. There is power is knowing you can tolerate frustration, that you don't have to act on impulse, that you can act in a way that is consistent with your top priorities, and not be daunted by even the most tantalizing distractions. There is strength in being able to distinguish between what is real and what is image, between what is truly nourishing and that which appears to be nourishing, between what is meant to be merely enjoyed and what is meant to be enjoyed **and** acted upon. At the very least, keeping your stress level within manageable proportions will make you live longer. The main drawback, however, is -- and it is a huge one -- being responsible may not feel good.

Exercise: Your Ideal Imaginary Other

By acquainting yourself with your fantasies, particularly who **your "ideal" imaginary other is and the unconscious emotional needs he or she represents,** you will:

- Better understand the link between the excitement you experience when you are attracted to someone and your emotional life.

- Be able to make a clearer distinction between your fantasies and reality.

- Be less likely to inflate the significance of sexual attraction.

- Become more aware of the unrealistic expectations you place on others, which will make you more accepting of others, especially when they are not what you want them to be.

- Recognize your own specific, unconscious, unmet emotional needs. As a result, you will be able to express them in your relationships. As your relationships become more satisfying, you will become less reliant upon your imagination.

- Learn about your "Achilles heel." Knowing where you are vulnerable will enable you to make healthier relationship choices.

- Be forced to depend more on yourself as an emotional resource.

The following is a visualization process of an encounter with your **ideal imaginary other**.

Relax. Breathe. With each exhalation, let go of the tension in your body. Clear your mind. Give yourself permission to enter the realm of your imagination, a realm that is limitless.

Free yourself to imagine whatever your heart desires. Notice if you hear any "I can'ts," or "I shouldn'ts" or "I'm not supposed tos" or anything else keeping you from total relaxation -- and let them go.

You're out with someone on a date. Pick a real person, someone you're sexually attracted to.

You notice that you're attracted. Take some time to notice what thoughts are going through your mind. How do you feel emotionally? What's happening in your body?

Do you let him or her know how you feel? If so, what do you say?

Is there anything you don't like? If so, how do you handle it?

You're conversing for hours. How does the conversation go? What do you say to each other?

You're getting more and more aroused. You make love. Imagine the scene. What was it that excited you most? How do you feel toward him or her, about having a relationship? Which emotional needs are getting met?

After completing this exercise, write down, in as much detail as possible, your answers to the questions asked.

CHAPTER ELEVEN

FOUR TYPES OF SEXUAL ATTRACTION

The fear singles talk most about is "attracting the wrong person." Knowing how to distinguish between healthy attraction and unhealthy attraction is a key concern.

There are four types of sexual attraction:

1) Pure fantasy
2) Projection of images
3) Projection of unconscious emotional needs
4) Sexual attraction as an outgrowth of intimacy

Pure Fantasy

Pure fantasy is probably the most common and innocuous type of attraction. It is a healthy expression of our sexuality as well as a healthy way to relieve frustration. It is safe and inconsequential because we don't have actual contact with the person we're fantasizing about. We can fantasize about someone anytime, anywhere, in the company of any person, and no one else knows that we're fantasizing.

Most of us don't realize the extent to which we fantasize. How often do we walk down the street, turn our heads and do a double-take of someone's body? How often are we in a work setting and hone in on another person's physical beauty or attractiveness? It can be the cashier, sales person, clerk, receptionist, doctor, accountant or client. Usually what happens is that someone we find physically appealing catches our eye, and our imagination does the rest. In that moment, we may idealize him or her as the "perfect partner." We may also imagine talking to, kissing or making love with this person. Virtually any scenario can happen in the imagination. Then, in a flash we are back to our real lives and on the way to our next destination.

Pure fantasy will likely have undesirable consequences when you don't know that you are fantasizing, can't accept the limitations of your imagination and act your fantasies out in an effort to make them reality. Certainly you don't want a fantasy to be the sole basis for initiating contact or pursuing a relationship.

Projection of Images

This type of sexual attraction occurs when emotionally charged images from a prior experience, such as a movie, book or memory, are projected onto someone we are attracted to, and we are not aware of making these projections. We are, in effect, relating to a figment of our imagination, not the person we're with. These projections are idealized images, the specific contents of which are an expression of unconscious emotional needs or wishes. They lie at the core of our motivation and become standards for what we expect real people and relationships to be.

For example, when I was fifteen years old, I read a pornographic story, *The Woman Next Door*. It was about an older, lovelorn woman, Mrs. Taylor, who seduced a teenager -- Billy. The story was told in graphic pornographic detail but in the guise of a love story. I had no idea that within the first five minutes of reading *The Woman Next Door*, I had put myself into Billy's shoes, and a relationship with Mrs. Taylor had already developed. For the next eight years or so, I saw or looked for Mrs. Taylor in every woman I was attracted to. All the while, the image of Mrs. Taylor was at the core of my motivation and molded my perceptions of women, relationships and intimacy.

Without question, the story spoke to my unconscious emotional needs. It was the way Mrs. Taylor acted. She responded to Billy like she really understood him, as if understanding was natural for her. I had never met anyone who was that understanding. Mrs. Taylor was the image of humanity I had been yearning for. She was everything I needed and wished for but never knew. At the time, although I wasn't aware of it, I was vulnerable because a variety of my emotional needs were not being met in my relationships. I needed to be seen, heard and known for who I was and what I was feeling. I needed validation and acceptance from a woman. I needed to feel wanted. I needed to feel special, like I made a difference in someone's life. I needed to be with a woman I could be vulnerable with, someone who wasn't going to reject me. I didn't really know anything about sex or women, and I didn't want to pretend that I did. I needed to be taught. But there was no one to teach me, until Mrs. Taylor came along.

Although I was looking for a real woman, my standard for "real" was an imaginary other, an ideal. Whenever I was in the company of a woman I was attracted to, I hoped and expected her to be like Mrs. Taylor or, at least, to act like Mrs. Taylor. When she fell short, as inevitably she would, I judged her as not good enough and not what I was looking for. No woman had a chance.

My first intimate relationship with a real person, Kathy, marked the beginning of the end of my relationship with Mrs. Taylor. It exposed the fallacy that was at the core of my experience with women. It taught me that it was in fact possible to be satisfied in a relationship with a woman who fell short of my ideal. I no longer relied on my imagination in the same way because I realized that my dream or ideal woman existed only in my fantasies and that no real person could ever be that way. Kathy became the new standard upon which my conceptions of women and relationships were based.

Projection of images is potentially dangerous for two main reasons. One is that what we are doing -- projecting images onto real people -- is happening unconsciously. The other is that people are not images. The reality is that no person or relationship will hold up against idealization. Problems often arise when our or our partner's humanness shows through. These problems range from doubts about oneself, the other person and the relationship to an inability to sustain a relationship.

Projection of Emotional Needs

Whenever we're with someone, our unconscious emotional needs are demanding, "What's in it for me?" These needs have a life of their own, molding our perceptions and motivating our behavior.

If we are attracted to someone and they say or do something that taps into an unconscious need, we might feel more attracted. If we are with someone we're not attracted to and this happens, we can suddenly find ourselves becoming attracted to him or her. In either case, the attraction is more emotionally based than sexually based.

When our **unconscious emotional needs** get met, it usually triggers a corresponding physical response. While we might be conscious of feeling sexually attracted, we remain unaware of what it is about him or her that turns us on. We will often attribute our attraction to other factors, such as character and compatibility, thereby distorting the quality of the relationship.

Projection of unconscious emotional needs is perhaps the most mystifying type of sexual attraction, because while we feel attracted and wish to be with this person, we are unaware of what is happening on an emotional level. This explains how we can find ourselves in a seemingly unlikely relationship or one in which after a relatively short period of time, we're wondering, "What am I doing with this person? How did I ever get involved with him or her?"

For example, you enter into a date not conscious of your need for acknowledgment (or any variation thereof, such as for another person to show interest or give attention, approval, appreciation). To compound matters, you've developed a deep sense of being undeserving of attention, which is also mostly unconscious. Your date is attentive and complimentary, perhaps overly so.

A common scenario is not consciously hearing or responding to the acknowledgment you've received. You're aware of wanting to see the person again, but you're not sure why, other than that you had a good time and were attracted to him or her. The voice of your unconscious needs would have been saying, "He or she is dynamite. He or she is what I want. I feel good. I want more of him or her."

Before long, you would be idealizing this person, selecting only desirable qualities while overlooking any undesirable ones and proceeding headlong into a relationship. Predictably, serious problems will arise on those occasions when these needs don't get fulfilled or when there is a conflict, at which time your perceptions of the person could change dramatically. "What's so good about him? He's not that attractive. He's not worth the trouble."

Let's reverse this situation. What if you respond to your date's acknowledgment of you with a profusion of gratitude, and this person is out of touch with his/her need to feel seen, heard, understood, etc.? She or he might "pedestalize" you and have thoughts like: "When was the last time anyone made me feel this good? He is the most wonderful, caring person I've met in a long time. I better pursue this." But when you fail to behave in the way she is accustomed to, her perceptions of you could suddenly turn negative.

Another example occurred in an interaction involving Troy and Adrienne. Adrienne became enraged because in her mind Troy had deceived her. Although Adrienne had good reason to be angry, the intensity of her reaction had more to do with her unconscious need for him to validate her so she would feel attractive and desirable.

When they were on their date, Troy seemed tired, disinterested and preoccupied. His low energy was confusing to Adrienne because they both had expressed an attraction and eagerness to get together again. In an effort to "pick the energy up," Adrienne decided to ask Troy whether he was attracted to her. Troy said he was.

The problem arose later, when Troy revealed that he had lied to Adrienne. He said that he actually felt unsure, and there probably wasn't a basis to pursue any type of relationship with her. It was Troy's belated honesty that caused her to feel mistrusting of him, humiliated and enraged.

In the process of exploring Adrienne's reactions to Troy, her unconscious emotional agenda was brought to light. When Troy first said he was attracted to Adrienne, he had fulfilled her underlying wish. But, when he was up-front about having misled her, he rescinded what she thought she had gotten from him. Because her need was for men to find her attractive and to want her was so strong, yet unconscious, she was looking for a particular response, not the truth. Adrienne's mistrust wasn't based so much on Troy violating her trust, but more on her need to count on his validation as "another feather in her cap." She was unaware of using him to bolster her own fragile sense of self-worth. Adrienne's primary motive wasn't, as it initially appeared, "to spice up the conversation."

Sometimes attraction as a projection of unconscious emotional needs occurs at the least expected times. For example, when Lois, a typist, was going over a manuscript with her client, Vince, Vince found himself becoming attracted to her. When Lois was in Vince's office reviewing manuscript changes, he noticed how hard she was trying to do a good job and please him. He suddenly became aware that his attention was no longer on the manuscript, but rather on her breasts.

The point is that Vince's unconscious emotional needs were activated. He felt special and taken care of because he, and his work, were important to Lois. He also felt powerful because she was doing exactly what he asked her to do. But, because he was able to shift his attention back to the purpose of the relationship -- the manuscript and Lois' typing -- he chose not to act on his feelings.

I have been awestruck at times when finding myself overwhelmed with desire, only to understand afterwards that my unconscious emotional needs had been tapped.

I have a very close platonic friend named Cindi whom I've been meeting for lunch a couple of times a month for the past several years. I've always considered her exceptionally attractive.

One of the times we met -- when she talked to me about her divorce -- I was beside myself with desire to go to bed with her. She shared her fears of having to stand up to her husband in court. In the seven years she had been married, she tried to be what she thought was a "good wife," avoiding conflict and rarely asserting herself. Now, in the process of settlement, she realized that if she didn't fight for what she felt was fair, she'd get burned.

She was being vulnerable with me, even more than usual. I responded naturally, as I would to any close friend who needed support and encouragement. I told her that the reason her marriage had become intolerable was that she was trapped in a role from which she couldn't break free. Standing up for herself without letting him make all these decisions for her would be unfamiliar territory, but it was a risk that she must be ready to take.

She responded by acknowledging how safe she felt opening up to me, what a close and special friend I was to her and how much she valued our relationship. This was when I began noticing my body getting aroused. It felt like I had just fallen in love. I thought about making love right then and there. I didn't want to leave. I didn't want it to be over. I wanted the feeling to last forever. Something had happened when she told me how much she appreciated me. I didn't know why or what.

The way I usually respond when I feel emotionally safe in a relationship is to share my experience at the moment. So I said to Cindi, "I wonder what is happening right now. Why is this conversation turning me on?" I asked. "Why is my body reacting so strongly? I didn't do anything out of the ordinary. I just told you what was obvious to me. You heard me. You appreciated my support, my love. I responded to you like I would to any close friend. What's the big deal?"

Then it dawned on me. We were relating on a deeper level than usual, a level in which my unconscious emotional needs were being tapped. Finally I was the hero I always wanted to be. I made a difference. I was important. Someone really appreciated me. Someone heard me. This is why such highly charged desire was suddenly ignited in me. Not only was I sexually excited, but my perception of Cindi and the nature of our relationship was became distorted in my mind. I began thinking, "Why am I with Barbara when I could have Cindi?"

It's not that I don't feel I'm important, appreciated and heard in my marriage -- I do. But wherever I am and whomever I'm with, I can't ignore the way it feels to be wanted and to be making a difference. In many ways, I live for it. I don't know if I could ever get enough of it. When I have this type of experience with a woman, I am usually aware of feeling closer, and this closeness feels all-encompassing. This feeling can and often does become physically and sexually arousing. What I have learned is that it's a special moment, not meant to be extended beyond its natural duration. It doesn't mean we should become lovers. It just means we have the ability to share our experiences, and the more personal we get, the better it feels.

Cindi and I said good-bye to each other, as we usually do, and went back to our respective lives.

Projection of unconscious emotional needs is potentially sabotaging because you are not aware of depending on your partner to make up for what you missed growing up. Some people will satisfy some of your needs some of the time, but no one will satisfy your needs all the time. What will you do -- what reason will you have to be in the relationship when you discover you are not going to get all you need (from your partner) and that the pain you are in is for you to deal with and for you to heal?

Being in touch with your needs enables you to maintain objectivity and not make choices that are based entirely upon the gratification derived from any one encounter. If you happen to get any of your unconscious needs met during a date, your awareness will prevent you from acting as if they were unconscious. It is less likely you will fall into the trap of idealizing the other person. You will have a much broader perspective of the person and the relationship. You will be able to think along the lines of: "I really like how this person made me feel. I definitely want to be with him (or her) again and see how it goes. Maybe this is a prelude to a relationship. But I won't know whether there's a basis for a relationship until we get to know each other a lot better -- so I better take it easy. Enjoy myself. Wait! Don't jump ahead! See how I feel when I'm not as excited. Don't assume there's more of a relationship than there is. One date, two dates, three dates, what does it matter? That's a spit in the ocean."

Sexual Attraction as an Outgrowth of Intimacy

The healthiest type of sexual attraction occurs when sexual attraction and emotional safety coexist. The two go together when there is rapport, when understanding is achieved, when you are relating to each other on a deep and personal level. In these situations, sexual attraction often evolves naturally.

The main difference between sexual attraction as a projection of unconscious emotional needs and sexual attraction as a natural response to being intimate is that in the latter case, we have an idea about what an intimate relationship entails and our decision to pursue a relationship is based on the existence of mutual interest, honesty and understanding. Our unconscious emotional needs are not the determining factor in our deciding to see that person again, getting more emotionally involved or pursuing a sexual relationship. Our ultimate satisfaction comes from sharing and connecting on a deeply personal level. It does not come from any one interaction, **even a particularly profound and sexually arousing one**. Nor does our ultimate satisfaction come out of interactions in which our unconscious emotional needs are being met.

For example, when Inga and Victor talked to each other about how they felt being together, they said the following:

> Inga: I'm very attracted to the qualities I see in you: your need to communicate your feelings and the way you live your life to the fullest. I appreciate when somebody causes me to look at how I'm leading my life, rather than just going down the road and never taking a look at where I'm going. I like it when I feel comfortable, putting it out the way I want to put it out. You challenged me in a way that I want and need to be challenged. I didn't feel afraid to stir up something that would cause an argument. I was able to disagree with you. We were able to fight. I can't stand to feel like I can't disagree or have conflict or when I'm afraid I might say something you're not going to like and won't tell me.

> Victor: I can talk to you, and we can exchange thoughts without my feeling that I'm going to be judged or told I'm wrong or what I mean. That kind of communication is essential. When I feel that you're open, I want to open up. I was able to talk to you about my ex-wife, feel that you understood me and you disagreed! We were able to disagree and still be respectful and caring towards each other, which is too significant to ignore.

Inga and Victor so appreciated being able to freely express themselves that they decided to pursue a relationship. Although initially they did feel a sexual attraction to each other, it was the depth and quality of their rapport that stimulated their desire for more contact. While they became more sexually attracted to each other toward the end of their date, their motivation for getting together was largely a result of having an impassioned disagreement. Emotional safety "turned them on."

Sexual attraction as an extension of intimacy often occurs in the context of work. Examples of this include the relationships actors have with fellow actors or that they have with directors; writers with agents, doctors with nurses, etc. -- they have intimate experiences working together. However, just because the relationship is intimate in a specific context doesn't mean it should automatically become sexual.

Let's take the relationship two actors have when they're working together. The nature of their work requires them to become emotionally naked with each other and with the audience. Each time they perform, their trust and sense of safety with each other builds. What happens to their relationship after the play is over, when they can no longer experience that sense of safety and accomplishment they shared with each other? It is often difficult for those in this situation to make the adjustment. The thought may cross their minds: "If we are intimate in this setting, we could be intimate in another setting. Love-making would be sublime," or something along the lines of: "Let's continue what we already have."

What would stop them from pursuing a relationship outside the professional domain? If they understood that their intimacy had occurred in the context of work and that pursuing intimacy in a different context is tantamount to starting all over again from the beginning, they might not be so inclined. They would still have to make the transition from the stage to real life. Take away the rehearsals, the excitement of performing for an audience, the depth of emotional expression when they're acting and the support from people around them -- what have they got? They are two people facing the same challenges as any other two people considering a relationship. They would have to spend some time together off stage to see whether there was a basis for an intimate relationship, and if there was, what kind of relationship would they want to have?

Distinguishing between these four types of sexual attraction should help to keep your priorities in order. You want your decision to pursue a relationship to be based primarily on the existence of intimacy -- mutual interest, honesty and understanding -- not excitement, imagination, need or anything else.

When we remember that our health and well-being are dependent on the nourishment we receive, it becomes clearer that **sexual attraction as an outgrowth of intimacy** is the way to go. The basic premise here is that relationships that are based on **images** and/or **needs** do not and will not provide the kind of nourishment we need. Intimate relationships are the ones that sustain us emotionally, mentally, physically and spiritually; the only ones that enliven, strengthen and uplift us; the ones that give meaning to our lives.

CHAPTER TWELVE

FOR YOURSELF, BY YOURSELF AND WITH YOURSELF

As long as you are "**alive**" -- in touch with your feelings, clear about your purpose and acting in a way that is consistent with that purpose -- **you will create intimate relationships.** Whether you are single and looking for an intimate partner or are in a quality relationship and want to keep it, staying alive is the key.

We are pulled, as if by magnetic forces, into contact with other human beings. However, what happens from the point of attraction -- how you relate, whether relationships materialize and the quality of the ones that do -- are functions of how connected you are to yourself. It is only when you are aware that your creativity makes it possible for you to turn what would otherwise be mundane, meaningless experiences into profoundly enlightening and gratifying encounters. The moment you lose that creative spark, intimacy becomes impossible.

It is when we are emotionally and spiritually depleted that the creative spark is so easily lost. Those times when frustration, apathy, fear and alienation set in the tendency is to try to go as far from reality as we can get. We resort to means that make us feel better, be it our imagination, psychological defenses (such as denial) or the endless assortment of means of escape at our disposal. If we continue to rely on these means, we become more isolated and desperate. We become oblivious to lack of human contact and understanding, oblivious to our health and well-being. We reach the point where we don't even know what being creative in our relationships means, nor do we care.

Staying alive in love or before we find love is a "chicken or egg" situation. We need inspiration to be creative and need to derive inspiration from what we create.

The ideal situation is when creativity **and** intimacy go together. Because relating to another human being intimately is emotionally and spiritually nourishing, the two naturally feed each other. The problem, however, is that we can't count on our encounters or relationships always being nourishing.

What do we do when love and intimacy are lacking? How do we enter into encounters nourished to begin with, and how do we sustain ourselves in the process? How do we sustain ourselves when our existing relationships fail to supply the nourishment we need? Where does our inspiration come from?

We must be able to be a source of nourishment for ourselves. We must have a relationship with ourselves. We must be intimate with ourselves.

What does having an intimate relationship with yourself mean?

It means treating yourself like a real live person. It means feeling worthy and capable of achieving your purpose in life. It means being aware of what is happening inside yourself on a feeling level. You talk to yourself about the situations you find yourself in. You ask yourself questions, and you answer them. You have ongoing conversations about what you need and what you need to do, and then you do it. The relationship you have with yourself is characterized by the same qualities as any intimate relationship: you **know**, **trust**, **accept** and **respect** yourself. These qualities must emanate from within before they can be shared with another person.

Unless you have role models or experience in intimate relationships (such as your parents' relationship with each other or your relationship with them), an intimate relationship with yourself does not come naturally. You need to make a conscious, concerted effort to develop one by honestly communicating about your feelings and needs whenever the opportunity presents itself, whether in the dating arena or in other relationships.

For example, let's take an experience I had recently in my relationship with Barbara that forced me to rely on myself. If I didn't have what I consider to be a strong relationship with myself, I probably would have acted in a way that would have, at the bare minimum, increased the level of stress in our relationship. At worst, I could have reacted in a way that threatened its very existence. Looking back, I'm glad I handled it the way I did.

With all of the day-in and day-out responsibilities of raising and providing for our family, it was a typically stressful time for us. She was caught up in her life. I was caught up in mine. Not only were we apart most of the time, when we were together, the children demanded attention. By the time we got them to bed, we were too tired to have any type of coherent conversation. Both of us were exhausted and just wanted to go to sleep. After a string of days like this, I began feeling estranged from Barbara. I felt neglected and hungry for more contact.

So what did I do? Tell her how I'm feeling, right? Being a therapist -- an intimacy and communication expert no less -- this comes naturally to me. I thought, expected and hoped that all I'd have to do is talk about how I was feeling, she'd change, and we'd feel close again. But this is not what happened.

After telling Barbara I was becoming increasingly dissatisfied and discontent because of her unavailability, things got worse. She interpreted what I said to mean that she wasn't a good enough wife, that she had fallen short, and that I was going to leave her because of it. In an effort to avoid the pain of what was in her mind the relationship's demise, she became more distracted and distant from me.

After this interaction, my negative feelings intensified and multiplied. In addition to feeling neglected and resentful, I felt misunderstood and helpless.

As pained as I was, the thought of ending the relationship never entered my mind. Nor did I question our love for each other. Rather, I backed off and went into myself. I was aware that what we were going through was, to a large extent, unavoidable, part of the process of life and relationship. Neither of us wanted it to be this way, but at that point, there was nothing we could do to change it. It wasn't the first time I (or she) felt this way, and it wasn't going to be the last. It was a tough time, but I knew it wasn't going to go on indefinitely. I trusted that we'd resume the conversation when we were both ready to do so, which eventually happened. When it did, a couple of days later, it was clear to both of us that we had been missing each other a lot and that we both wanted the same thing -- to get some time alone together, which we made sure we did.

In this situation, my relationship with myself served me in a number of ways. I **trusted** myself enough to act on how I felt, to take a risk. Rather than stuffing my feelings or feeling wrong for having them, which would have been easy to do because they were uncomfortable, I made an effort to communicate to Barbara. I remember moments when I tried to talk myself out of my feelings and rationalize them away: "It's just a rough period we're going through. It's no one's fault. Barbara isn't intentionally hurting me. If I say anything, her feelings might be hurt, which would only make matters worse." As it was, I sat with these feelings for over two weeks.

I **knew** myself. I knew that I loved Barbara and at the same time I knew I was quite resentful and angry. I knew why I was angry: because some of my needs for attention and affection were not getting met. I wanted more contact and to feel closer physically and emotionally. I had no intention of leaving Barbara or hurting her. Nor did I doubt that she or our relationship was "right" or good enough. I was able to see that the way she reacted to me initially had to do with prior relationship. My communication to Barbara was **unconditional**. I knew that at the core of my communication was the yearning for closeness and understanding. My self-esteem did not hinge on her response. I really didn't have any idea how she was going to respond. Regardless of her response, it was not going to pose a threat to how I felt about myself or our relationship. I believe that my physical, emotional, mental and spiritual well-being is ultimately my responsibility.

Barbara's reaction obviously wasn't what I had hoped for. I didn't get what I wanted, and I had to wait even longer before any resolution. Initially, I was enraged. I was, however, able to deal with my anger because I had a "home" in myself -- a place to go to and wait until Barbara and I were in a calmer, clearer frame of mind to resume the conversation. If I wasn't truly comfortable being with myself, I wouldn't have had anywhere to go. Chances are, I would have acted out of desperation, which likely would have been detrimental to myself as well as to our relationship. I was able to grant Barbara some time and space to respond **in her own way, when she was ready to**. I also believe that if I weren't accepting of my own struggles, imperfections and limitations, I would not have been able to tolerate Barbara's.

My experience brings attention to the key aspect in creating and sustaining intimate relationships: **our relationship with ourselves**. It is this relationship that determines the quality of all of our other relationships. How we act when we are challenged -- when we find ourselves in situations we would prefer to avoid but can't -- is what makes or breaks a relationship; and how we act is a function of the quality of the relationship we have with ourselves.

Although relationships are integral to your growth and well-being, they are limited. While there are some basic needs that should get met in an intimate relationship, such as the need for understanding and caring, there are many needs that go unmet. No one can make you feel totally satisfied and secure.

The irony is that when one need gets met, another pops up. One minute you may feel perfectly contented with your partner. The next you may feel completely disgusted. This is why you must be able to rely on yourself to get through the tough times and to turn difficult situations into opportunities for growth. When you are angry, hurt, vulnerable, helpless, confused, disappointed, frustrated or alone, you must care for yourself. Ultimately, you are the best friend you've got!

APPENDIX

After ten years as an addiction specialist, I've come to recognize that unhealthy, nonintimate relationships are the spawning ground of addiction. I've noticed that after the primary treatment objective has been achieved (a sustained period of abstinence), a successful recovery depends on the recovering addict's ability to develop a support system of healthy, intimate relationships.

Yet many people -- including those who are addiction-free -- lack the experience and skills necessary to make intimacy possible. This poses a tremendous clinical challenge.

The therapeutic relationship is often the recovering addict's first experience in a healthy relationship. In theory, this relationship acts as a springboard toward the development of other healthy relationships. The client is supposed to "bring the inside out." Unfortunately, I have learned that it does not always work this way -- for several reasons.

First, the quality of the therapeutic relationship is not the primary determinant of change. Most critical is the client's level of motivation to apply what he or she has learned in therapy to real-life situations. I tell my clients that "therapy is what happens when you leave my office." It is the client's experience in handling relationships outside of the relationship with the therapist that will ultimately change how a person thinks, feels and acts.

Even with my most motivated clients, however, the impact of the therapeutic relationship is limited. The client-therapist relationship is, in many respects, idealized. When relating in the real world, clients don't get the same sense of unconditional acceptance as they do in therapy.

Furthermore, upon leaving therapy, clients somehow have to learn to communicate effectively in a sea of dysfunction. They must learn how to swim or else drown. For those who have never experienced a healthy relationship prior to entering therapy, and even for those who have, developing intimate relationships in the "real world" presents a monumental challenge.

The Dating-to-Relate Workshop

Based on my belief that the therapy or learning process is accelerated by "bringing the outside in," I created a workshop that focuses entirely on how the participants deal with real-life relationship situations -- dating. I called the workshop **Dating to Relate**. (Many of the examples presented throughout this book were taken directly from a number of **Dating to Relate** workshops I conducted.)

The structure of **Dating to Relate** combines "blind dates" (or "**practice dates**") and "**second encounters**." The "**second encounters**" occur when the whole group is together. They involve dialogue between those who have "dated" -- giving and receiving feedback about their experience together.

This format makes it possible for the participants to explore issues that typically arise in dating situations, but frequently are not acknowledged by the daters themselves. Issues most commonly addressed include sexual attraction and it's lack, honesty and its lack, preconceived notions, expectations, insecurities, conflicts, differences, judgments and ambivalence. By discussing thoughts and feelings they be concealing or unaware of, participants are able see how they affect and are affected by others. During this process I point out relationship-sabotaging behavior and demonstrate effective communication skills that participants practice right then and there. In so doing, they gain experience that enables them to change their behavior in relationship situations outside of the workshop.

In each heterosexual workshop there are eight participants -- four men and four women. Participants are carefully screened to determine their level of motivation, as well as their potential to derive benefit from the workshop. (While this book addresses only heterosexual "dates," the **Dating to Relate** workshop was created for a variety of different populations, including gay men, lesbians, teenagers, seniors and physically and emotionally disabled people. The principles of healthy dating and communication apply to people and relationships in general and are not limited to heterosexual adults.)

I ask participants to abide by several basic rules. Each date consists of a minimum of two hours of relating without the distraction of movies, plays, parties, etc. I recommend activities such as walks, dinner or going out for coffee. During the workshop and dating encounters, with the exception of cigarettes and coffee, there is to be no use of any mind or mood-altering substances, such as marijuana or alcohol. There are to be no sexual encounters. Chemicals and sex are often means used to escape the anxieties dating elicits. Because these anxieties are a natural part of the process of becoming intimate, participants face them so they can learn to deal with them.

The question "Do the approaches applied in the **Dating to Relate** workshop readily transfer to 'real' dates?" is often raised. The answer is that while the "dates" are part of a therapy workshop, and therefore might seem contrived and unreal, the situations and issues that arise are very real. The same or similar situations are common in dating and occur in all stages of relationships. How participants react and communicate represent generalized patterns. The unconscious sabotaging baggage they bring to encounters is the same baggage they bring to real-life situations. Furthermore, because the focus is on **how**, rather than **who**, we date and relate to, by dating others they wouldn't ordinarily date, participants are in a position to see how natural and creative they are just being with another person.

Some people feel that the no-sex policy makes the "dates" unreal. Again, the imposed structure does make the dates different from actual dating situations. However, the purpose of setting these parameters is to examine the behavior and motivation that shape relationship experiences in the real world.

For example, if one or both partners feel sexually attracted on their date, the no-sex policy forces them to become more aware of their feelings and how they tend to act in these situations. It also allows them time and space to assess quality of rapport, ability to communicate and whether having sex would be beneficial. Because, in actual dating situations, sexual feelings are often acted out in order to avoid real contact, this rule also works to bring anxieties and insecurities that might otherwise be deflected to the fore.

You may have difficulty accepting some of the examples in this book as common occurrences because you may not have ever had such experiences, and you may never have them. However, you don't have to relate to all the examples in the book in order to learn from them. Rather, look at your own experiences and see how the underlying principles can be applied. As you learn and apply these basic principles, you will notice subtle changes -- particularly in how creative you are, how well you communicate and in the quality of your relationships.

To preserve anonymity, the names of **Dating to Relate** workshop participants have been changed.

Below is what some **Dating to Relate** participants said about why they took the workshop.

> Kaila: I'm forty-four years old and have never been married. I would like to understand the male psyche more. I don't think I correctly interpret what a man wants. I've not been in a romantic relationship and have had only friendships.
>
> I feel comfortable with the concept of dating but get uncomfortable when I'm actually with someone on a date...with a stranger. I remember one date which made me think. This man told me that I had a wall up. I felt that he was on target. I didn't know that I was holding men at arm's length. I don't want to do that anymore.

Dirk: I'm forty-seven years old, married and divorced twice. My professional life has gone along really well, but what is more important, my relationships have not.

I think that I have a pattern of taking care of women because I've found myself staying in relationships that I didn't really want just so I would not hurt the person.

When I feel good about myself, dating is fun. It is interesting to get to know someone new -- when I don't feel any pressure. When I'm feeling badly about myself, I'm trying desperately to be liked. So, when I date, I often find myself going back and forth between pleasure and desperation.

June: I'm forty years old and have never been married. I've done a lot of dating, had a lot of short relationships. I've been successful in my career and have a wonderful network of friends but haven't established a long-term relationship.

I want to learn how to relate more openly and honestly when I'm dating. I tend to hold back from saying anything negative or anything I think will hurt the other person's feelings. I don't want to give the impression of "not being nice" or of being critical. I'm also aware of lacking direction, because my tendency is to let the man take the lead. If he's open, then I'll be more open. If he's not, then I won't be.

Mat: I'm thirty-seven years old, married fifteen years and have two kids. When I got divorced, I did what we do when we are twenty-one years old; that is, what I call "serial monogamy." I've been with women, one after the other, and sleep with them without a relationship ever materializing. I'm clueless about the whole process of getting to know someone, and I want the opportunity to practice because I've never really dated.

Toby: I'm thirty-eight years old, have never been married and have no children. I come from an alcoholic family where my father reigned over the rest of us. From an early age, I stayed away from men from fear they'd be like my dad. The only way I was able to go out with men was to get "loaded" first. I didn't know how not to get myself into abusive relationships. I finally recognized that I am an alcoholic and am in recovery at this time. I'm not dating. I don't know how to date. I need to learn about intimacy in a nonsexual way.

Cary: I'm thirty-three and have never been married. I didn't do any dating until after college. The dating I have done since has been sporadic -- maybe ten dates in the last ten years. I know that my self-worth has been virtually nonexistent. The relationships I tried to develop didn't work. The last one was particularly painful, and because of it I entered therapy. I'm just now in therapy, learning to talk about my feelings. I haven't any idea about what a healthy relationship consists of or the skills necessary to create one.

Dear Reader,

I hope you found the insights and life stories in this book valuable. Assuming that you apply the principles presented in this book I would like to hear how they worked for YOU, as well as comments, questions and powerful learning experiences you've had.

. . . .

Hylen Publishing
935 Lootens, Suite 208
San Rafael, California 94901

☐ Please send me _____ copy(s) of *Dating, A Guide To Creating Intimate Relationships*. $13.95 each. (Price includes shipping and handling and California sales tax.)

> **Discounts:**
> Orders of 10 or more: 10% off cover
> Orders of 50 or more: 20% off cover
> Orders of 100 or more: 30% off cover
> Orders of 200 or more: 40% off cover

☐ Please send me information regarding your schedule of events (lectures, workshops, etc.).

☐ Please send me information about scheduling a lecture or workshop for my group.

Name _____

Address _____

City _____ State _____ Zip _____

Phone(s)   home (_____) _____

            work (_____) _____